Victor Vrublevski

Security or electronic concentration camp?

Persons` identification techniques, errors, consequences

Anchor Academic
Publishing

Vrublevski, Victor: Security or electronic concentration camp? Persons` identification techniques, errors, consequences, Hamburg, Anchor Academic Publishing 2014

Buch-ISBN: 978-3-95489-268-6
PDF-eBook-ISBN: 978-3-95489-768-1
Druck/Herstellung: Anchor Academic Publishing, Hamburg, 2014

Bibliografische Information der Deutschen Nationalbibliothek:
Die Deutsche Nationalbibliothek verzeichnet diese Publikation in der Deutschen Nationalbibliografie; detaillierte bibliografische Daten sind im Internet über http://dnb.d-nb.de abrufbar.

Bibliographical Information of the German National Library:
The German National Library lists this publication in the German National Bibliography. Detailed bibliographic data can be found at: http://dnb.d-nb.de

© Anchor Academic Publishing, Imprint der Diplomica Verlag GmbH
Hermannstal 119k, 22119 Hamburg
http://www.diplomica-verlag.de, Hamburg 2014
Printed in Germany

DECISION AND RISK AT IMMIGRATION SERVICE WORK

The aim of the paper:

- to distinguish the factors decreasing the risks while taking decision.

The tasks of the paper:

- to define risk factors;
- to analyse how risk influences on decision taking;
- to discern risk decreasing factors;
- to apply risk decreasing factors in practice.

Risk factors:

- Poor reading skills;
- Poor writing skills;
- A lot of information and its poor arrangement;
- Huge bureaucracy, formalities, responsibility;

ANNOTATION

The research is titled "Decision and risk at law immigration service work." This paper consists of *79* pages, *7* divisions, *6* subdivisions, *36* tables (*29*-designed by the author), *9* figures (*5*-designed by the author), *1* picture and *73* references. The author of the paper has analysed different sources, such as scientific studies and publications, textbooks, science journals and the books referred to the possible consequences of decision taking. In his practical part of the paper, the author has compared consequences of decisions which could be taken by a lower rank official working in immigration service. The author has chosen the topic because he discerns the controversy between a great number of information and its poor arrangement at the Immigration service. As a result, a lot of time should be spent to take a decision and meanwhile its quality decreases.

CONTENT

PREFACE

Research novelty: the research links up probability, risk theories with their practical application at immigration service work;

Aim of the research: to find out risk diminishing factors taking a decision at immigration service work;

Object of the research: immigration service;

Subject of the research: risk diminishing factors;

Base of the research: immigration service officials;

Tasks of the research:

1) to find out risk factors;

2) to analyse risk impact on decision making;

3) to define risk diminishing factors;

4) to put into practice risk diminishing factors.

Research methods:

The theoretical ones: to analyse references and service documentation;

The practical ones: observation, surveys, experiments, analysis.

Questions of the research:

1) What is decision?

2) What can influence decision taking?

3) Which is the best decision?

4) Which are the reasons and consequences of incorrect decision?

Theoretical model and references used:

Juridical, mathematical, technical references were used including: books on probability, risk, and decision taking theories, systemization and logic.

Hypothesis of the research:

Systematization of actions may reduce the probability to take incorrect decisions at immigration service work.

8

CHAPTER 1

Each decision deliberately taken is always a choice from variety of possible decisions. Each decision, in its turn, brings consequences: positive or negative. If these consequences are known in advance, the tactic is very simple — to choose the decision which will lead to the targeted results or consequences. Unfortunately, it is not always possible to predict consequences of the decision taken.   According   to   the decision theory, various options we choose are called alternatives. So, if the decision "A is better than B, and B is better than C, then logically that "A is better than C" (33, 13). These alternatives may also be expressed by numbers or by words, such as if we „ assign to A the value 15, to B the value 13 and to C the value 7" and since "A has a higher number than either B or C, A should be chosen." (33, 13).

Even if the best decision has been taken, it can be hard to prove or express in numbers its quality or value. For example the expression "A is better that B" is "binary relation" (33, 14) because it is impossible to define how much A is better then B? Another good example could be "a cup of coffee and sugar". For example there are 1000 cups of coffee where "C0 –cup has no sugar, C1 – one grain of sugar, up to C999 !" (33, 19) A man drinking coffee from both cups C0 , C1 „can not taste the difference" (33,19) in one granule and the coffee in both cups will taste for him as without sugar. The opposite situation will occur when comparing coffee from cups C0, C1 with the cup C999. In the latter case Hoffman will be able to feel the sugars and "clearly taste the difference" (33, 19). Clearly there exists some sensitivity threshold - Cx which depends on the number of sugar granules. If there are less than x sugar granules in the cup the person will not distinguish its presence and will consider such coffee without any sugar and vice versa. The threshold may vary for different people and even sometimes does not exist at all when, for example, one is ill with agnosia an illness characterized with the loss of taste functions of the tongue, or "inability to taste." (44, 368). When for example, we say to our child "the weather today was better than yesterday and you may leave umbrella at home" it is not necessary to compare physical qualities of cyclone like wind speed, pressure, moisture. In our daily life we can evaluate many things approximately and it is enough to understand each other without any numbers or formulas, but there are cases when precise data is essential. No one would argue that precise data is the basis of such sciences as mathematics, physics, mechanics, but what about jurisdiction? How to define in which indices it is possible to measure the good or bad decision?

Each decision depends on some conditions, for example there are two alternatives for a man: to take or not take an umbrella before leaving home? Here the main condition on which the decision taking will depend is if it "rains or it does not rain." (33, 25) Rain is here risk factor. After having taken the decision one may predict and expect possible outcomes or consequences of this decision, for example, if an official takes the decision he too must predict possible risks, choose an appropriate decision and after all taking responsibility for it. Let us try to measure decisions and their outcomes on the example of "umbrella and rain." (33, 25) So, if someone has taken an umbrella with him, but the rain will not pour that day, in turns out that there is no rain but his suitcase is heavier. And opposite, if someone has not taken an umbrella but there is a heavy downpour – his suitcase is lighter but he will be totally wet. One can conclude that the ideal opportunity for such person would be an easy suitcase and no rain! Let us describe all possible decisions and their outcomes in the following table which in scientific slang is called "decision matrix." (33, 25)

Table No.1.1. **Possible outcomes in situation "to take or not to take an umbrella"** (33, 25)

	it rains	it does not rain
umbrella	dry clothes, heavy suitcase	dry clothes, heavy suitcase
no umbrella	soaked clothes, light suitcase	dry clothes, light suitcase

Then let us "value" (33, 26) these outcomes in the scale from 1 to 10, where 10 is the best and most suitable, desirable outcome. As it has been written before the best opportunity for a person, especially a woman, is to go out in a sunny morning without an umbrella and therefore let us mark this opportunity with 10 and, on the contrary, no one would like to be under a heavy downpour without an umbrella. (See the following table)

Table No.1.2. **possible outcomes in situation "to take or not to take an umbrella"**
expressed with numbers in 10 point value scale. (33, 26)

	it rains	it does not rain
umbrella	5	5
no umbrella	1	10

* the values in the table are introduced by the author

In the example of rain and umbrella it was possible, at least approximately, to define outcomes and even to determine their probability, but there exist decisions where one will not be able to predict their outcomes and therefore they are called decisions under "non-certainty." (33, 26) Each event, according to the probability theory may occur with probability from zero to one or in other words from 0% to 100%. In the example of "rain and umbrella" it is acceptable to define possible outcomes and their probability. In our case the probability of being wet or dry will greatly depend on wind, moisture in the atmosphere and if one wishes one can find out quite accurate weather forecast in his region for a particular time. The fact is that there are decisions which may cause unpredictable outcomes like: will my deposit bring profit or loss in two years; will the sportsman win or lose competition, etc.

An official must always try to foresee possible outcomes of his decision because on this will depend someone's health and sometimes even life. If all possible outcomes of a decision were evident the problem could be solved easily-choose the decision which will be correct, suitable, profitable, but unfortunately or fortunately there are also decisions which will be taken under non-certainty, then the law may sound as follows: the more one knows or the more information one possess on the object, the better one can predict its future behavior. In our daily language we usually describe the probability of some event with ordinary words and phrases like: certainly, unlikely, sure. (See the next table)

Table No.1.3. **Scale of knowledge situations and decision problems (33, 28).**

certainty	deterministic knowledge
risk	complete probabilistic knowledge
uncertainty	partial probabilistic knowledge
ignorance	no probabilistic knowledge

If someone is certain of something that means that he possesses exhaustive information on something and due to it he is able to predict its future behavior with the highest possible degree. For example, rocket designers and engineers know their constructed objects or systems almost in detail and it is compulsory in order to be convinced that during the real flight the object will function according to the calculated characteristics. Otherwise, the less one knows about an object the worse will be one's prediction degree.

The ability to predict is necessary not only for engineers, but also for officials. For a policeman it is important to know if a detainee will assail or not, will he escape or not, will he submit or not, etc. If one could certainly predict the above-mentioned problems they would be solved simply: it is compulsory to put handcuff-because the detainee will assail, it is compulsory to put him behind the bars-because he will escape, but due to the lack of information about the detainee one can never certainly predict his future behavior. Though one hundred percent probability degree is a theoretical value, some events are predictable to the degree close to 100% and due to such a high number they may be considered certain in occurrence.

From author's point of view, probability degree is conditional value because each seemingly inevitable event may not happen due to the possible but. For example, if one throws a stone-it will definitely land, but only if Earth's gravity does not diminish, if there is no atomic blast at the moment of the up-throw, etc. Evidently these but will never be taken into calculation of many formulas, like path of projectile, but nevertheless their possible appearance and influence will make the formula absurd.

Our human language, mathematics is incapable of explaining some natural events. For example, "an event with probability of 0,000001 (one chance in a million) is a rather an unlikely event" (19, 14), but from psychological point of view, people dealing with the event which appears with probability of 0,000001 will be so accustomed to its absence that will eventually qualify it as impossible. Furthermore, humankind helplessly struggles to describe events in the grand scheme of things, where due to universal domains "distinctions of any kind become impossible." (16, 99) But nevertheless being curious by nature, humans try to use available, restricted methods of their imperfect science to explore a boundless and perfect universe.

Let us return to the earth, in order to exclude risks from assault the law allows policemen to use handcuffs and other special means. In case of need a policeman will choose from two possible options: to put or not to put handcuffs. Here, decision taking process is fast and almost entirely depends on detainee's behavior and health condition.

A process of decision taking may extend and become far more complicated in the cases when a number of detainees increase, if they are in different places, they have committed various crimes, they are speaking different languages. In such complicated condition sophisticated computer based systems, particularly "decision-making program" (35, 179) may be effectively applied. There exist various systems of that kind, but if an official is a manager he can choose "information reporting system, decision support system and executive information systems" to "facilitate rapid and effective decision making," (18, 291) The above-mentioned systems differ in amount of data stored, their aim, but the common feature is that they process information, then provide answers. Main function of decision systems may be expressed in the chain "if-then": if you do this, then the consequences will be these." The application of decision-making systems is preferable in the cases when there is a lot of data which must be processed quickly, but accurately. For example, some law enforcement institutions in the USA apply "computer-aided dispatch systems or CAD" (43, 74) to provide effective management of victim-police chain. The role of CAD system is so great that it is even "in the core of police departments` decision support process!" (43, 74)

SUBCHAPTER 1.1

Decision is "usually understood to be synonymous with choice" (13, 1), but sometimes it may be dangerous to choose. At his work an official also has to choose one alternative among others which in the end will be his decision he will be responsible for. American scientist Bruce F. Baird writes that every decision taken may influence taker's "reputation" far in the future. (12, 5) As it has been written in the previous part, more often one has to take decision under uncertainty where one can not absolutely predict its outcomes, but nevertheless one has to work and take decisions. In order to organize this process, not only computer software, but morphological analysis is used as well.

Let us take a look at decision making from the standpoint of combinatorial analysis. For example, a manager has to divide three prizes: award, appreciation, cash bonus among his 6 juniors. According to the "permutation" it can be done in 6*5*4=120 different combinations! (42, 2) More likely that an ordinary manager due to the overload, lack of time or simply idleness, does not consider even the tenth part of these combinations, but rather keeps in mind his best subordinates and distributes the prizes according to their merits. In the above-mentioned problem a manager may calculate all possible variations or choose several ones, but in the end particular decision must be taken and it will be judged by its consequences or "final result" (12, 14).

The above-mentioned example of distributing prize is an illustrative one because in practice it is difficult to imagine a manager considering all 120 variations according to the combinatorial theory. Finally there may be and there are real situations when manager has to find and analyse all possible variations seriously.

How can an ordinary manager consider all variations or how he can orient himself in the sea of numbers and permutations when combinatorial theory and math may have been forgotten by him since school times? One of the ways in which to expose variations luminously is decision tree. (See the next figure) In it one can see all possible actions relating to the particular decision, let us analyse official's decision-to detain a foreigner.

Figure No. 1.1.1. **Decision tree**

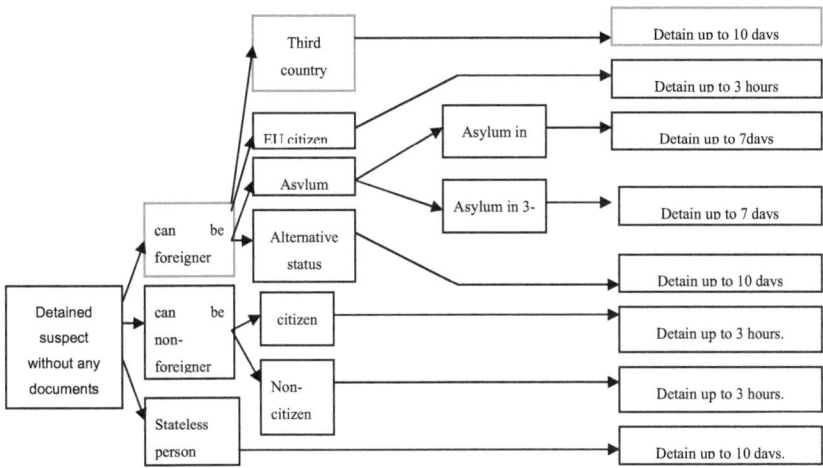

* the tree designed by the author

The above-exposed decision tree is in shortcut form because the rightmost decision to "detain" is not the final one and decision chain could have been continued with the following, sequential actions: to frisk person, his belongings-write protocol-inform authorities-to put into detention facilities... The tree is an illustrated summary of possible officials' actions and is very convenient from pedagogical point of view. If the tree is considered from probability theory's point of view, it may look like as follows:

Figure No. 1.1.2. **Decision tree and probability theory**

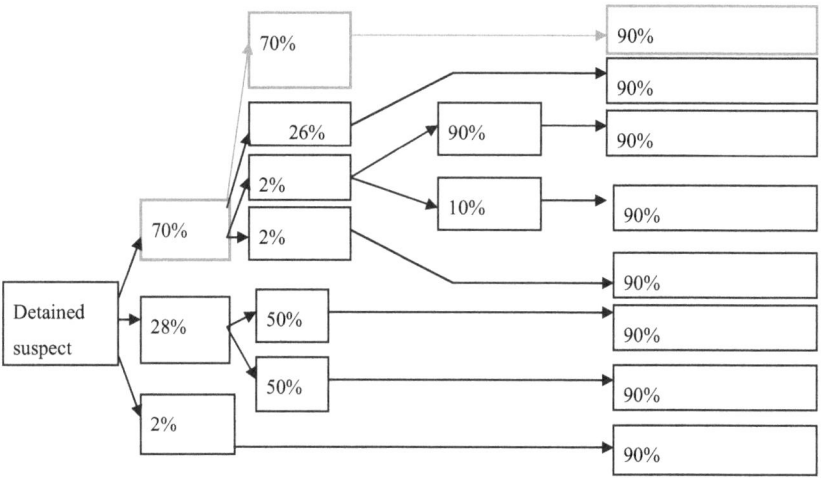

* The tree designed by the author

This tree is equivalent to the previous one except for the number of probability degree inside its boxes. Each box represents an approximate probability of the action which the author drew from his own statistic data. So, with the probability of 70% the detained suspect without any travel documents will be a foreigner, with the same probability he will be the third country national and finally according to the immigration law he will be almost certainly detained up to 10 days (90%), but if he has relatives in the country or is very ill, detention can be replaced with the regular checking at the police office (10%). The chain of actions (marked with green) will occur more often in immigration policeman's work and one may even predict that the suspect without any travel document will be the third country national who will be detained for certain.

Decision tree is a convenient way of graphical summarization of laws, operating instructions because on the page one can see permitted actions, their probability and finally it discharges user from reading the original text. The last circumstance is very essential in society where people read less and less and therefore their reading skills decrease from generation to generation. Reading is not only a pronunciation of words, but acquisition of visual information from the page and its "comprehension" (58, 23) Contemporary generation generally became used to the information such as advertisement, short, adopted texts. Characteristic property of adapted materials is that it is deliberately designed to "catch the reader's attention." (57, 113) It is possible to arrange actions not only on the paper, but in the software too. The software is convenient if:

- one needs to find out *all* possible actions *immediately*.

One of the software composing decision trees is "SAS Enterprise Miner" or Statistical Analysis System". (37) As some contemporary software, it has auxiliary functions including drawing decision trees of various degrees and complexity. In other words, SAS is an electronic decision tree, but additionally each decision tree's operational mode contains "if-then" development. (14, 265)

SUBCHAPTER 1.2

In order to calculate the risk factors decision taker needs two things: "a probability estimate and a consequence/impact estimate." (26, 73) Probability degree may be represented by numbers from 0- the event will never happen, to 1- the event will happen with probability 100%. Possible consequence, or better to say, impact is also expressed with numbers from 0 to 1. In order to assess risk one needs to correlate both probability and impact/damage and there is the formula for this purpose: "event probability x probability of damage." (4, 45) For example, the door is created to enter and leave the flat and if someone nevertheless decides to go out through the window of the third floor the probability that he will fall down is one and damage caused by falling down could be serious- 0,8. According to the above-mentioned formula, the risk of going out through the window here is 1 x 0,8 = 0,8 or 80%. If a hundred percent is the highest possible number of risk, then 80% is sufficient reason to use the door for this purpose.

Damage's evaluation with numbers is a convenient and accurate method to compare risks because in a daily work, the officials are not supposed to calculate risk at the regular basis and usually they compare risk intuitively or approximately. Wordy risk assessments do not contain precise data therefore the latter one is substituted by standard phrases like "drastic consequences," "high risk", "may endanger security" and often such assessments are accepted as admissible in official reports when in practice there is "no possibility of calculating probability or determining real impact without using data." (32, 86) Though a wordy risk assessment is an inaccurate and general one, nevertheless, it may remain the only possible and accessible humanly transparent method for those who do not know math. Risk assessment formula can be widely used for different situations. In the table below, using risk assessment formula, one can see a probable impact for an official in a particular situation.

Table No.1.2.1. **Risk assessments for an official missing his job and risk assessments when he does not explain a detainee his rights.**

Official's violation	probability of particular consequence (in words)	probability of particular consequence (0-1)	damage brought by particular consequence (in words)	damage brought by particular consequence (0-1)	Risk assessment = risk probability x damage x 100
To be late for job for 2 minutes	minimal	0,1	minimal	0,1	1%
Not to come to the job	high	0,95	considerable	0,6	57%
Not to explain to the detained foreigner his rights	high	0,8	notable	0,9	72%

the table designed by the author

For example, if an official misses job for two minutes the consequences of this violation are not expected to be severe and there is a minimal probability that his chief will notice it. In excuse of his delay the employee may provide the proof that the time on his and chief's clock may differ for several minutes. Then let us mark the probability that the chief will notice official's delay as 0,1 or 10% and possible damage- reproof from the chief also as 0,1 and according to the formula, risk level is here 0,01 or 1%. And

18

otherwise, absence from work without reasonable excuses will be definitely noticed by the chief and he will therefore punish his subordinate severely. "The probability of an event is equal to the sum of probabilities of its component outcomes." (8, 13) And it can be scored by formula: P (A) = m – occurrence of the particular event / n – summary of all events occurred or P (A) =m/n. And possible damage of an event may be defined arbitrary in the range from 0 to 1.

As a result there will appear quite precise risk level assessment for a particular situation, but in order to make it more precise it is important to accumulate data on damage, probability. This accumulation is called statistic and the more data accumulated the more precise will be risk assessment itself. In order to prove the previous statement one should turn to the classical example of heads or tails. Which event will dominate over – appearance of heads or tails? It is proven that in this case probability of both events will be approximately the same-50%. But if a coin has been flipped comparatively not many times, for example 100 times, then it may be that the occurrence of head "is 44 times." (11, 68) And here the law is "the more you toss the coin, the nearer the outcome will be to the predicted probability" of 50%. (49, 33).

The probability of two similar events and possible damage (outcome) degree will various in different working places, but nevertheless risk assessment is an appropriate way to characterize decision. If we flip coin three times it can happen that eagle occurs two times and the tail one time, but it does not follow thence that eagle's probability degree is 66,66%! This example clearly demonstrates why accumulation of data makes prediction more precise, but here arises another question - how much data must be accumulated to derive a probability degree of an event? The answer is indefinite, but the tendency is evident - "the more experiments are conducted the average value obtained in the n experiments should approach the expected value." (67, 183) Therefore, tossing a coin three times or is not enough to derive even approximate probability of occurrence of head and tail (see the next table).

Table No. 1.2.2. **Tossing of a coin.** (70, 28)

Number of flipped coins-n	Occurrence of head-m (times)	P(head) occurrence probability % = m/n x 100
10	4	40 %
100	42	42 %
1000	460	46 %
10000	4950	49,5 %

An official may as well use the risk assessment formula in his work to define detainees' breakup probability, possible damage, nationalities involved in it etc. The question of whether risk assessment should be conducted by an official or specially trained colleagues remains secondary one, but nevertheless the author of the paper insists on a separate division or office responsible for data accumulation and further assessment of probability, damage and risk because an official or a policeman must be fully occupied with his direct duties and not with mathematical estimation. Theoretically, the final product of risk assessment performed by this office could be new service instruction based on risk, probability and decision-making theory. The outstanding characteristic of such instruction could be its scientific basis.

SUBCHAPTER 1.3

One of many reasons, but probably the decisive one why most people solve problems unsuccessfully is an "unstructured approach" to solution. (53, 11) Distinctive feature of this approach is "chaos and randomness." (53, 12) Having analysed people who resolved problems successfully the researchers G. Nadler and W. Chandon concluded that they applied asking smart questions. This approach to solution is not a scientific breakthrough in methodology because even an ancient Greek philosopher and thinker Socrates practiced it and so "infuriated" (53, 16) representatives of authorities with it that they sentenced him to death in the end.

This method may indeed irritate ordinary users because it presents a challenge and extra mental job therefore it drastically differs from habitual, template way of solving problems. Template thinking is far less energy and time demanding than the critical one since it is often supported from our habits. For example, there are numerous absurd things which are accepted, approved and even mandatory in society. In records management it is polite to write "yours respectively" at the bottom of the letter, but what if I despise the addressee or do not know him personally? How can I respect a person whom I have neither seen nor spoke with? The second example, it is almost a common legal procedure when a chief shall be released from position if any of his subordinates commits service violations. How on earth can one man who is sitting in the office be responsible for all his subordinates' actions? One more example, there is a standard routine in paperwork when the head of an office signs blank sheets of certificates, letters of acknowledgment and other supportive documents in advance and it is recognized that the chief himself has awarded the top performer. Usually it is the clerical office which compares performance results, proposes top candidates and brings documents for signature. As a result the habit to perform absurd actions does not contribute to the development of critical thinking. Apparently there are numerous examples of unexplainable logic in legal documents therefore many service instructions may contain such "mandatory absurd" as well. In their work, officials are supposed to trust and follow service instructions which may subsequently cause excessive "dependence" (66, 112) on them. The author does not deny the necessity of instructions at all, but in non-routine situations only critical thinking may be indispensable. Let us analyse and see it in the following examples:

Situation No.1. Car driver while driving a car in a remote place pierced his front tire. The first expected question is-where is spare wheel and jack to pick up the car and replace the wheel? But if there is no jack inside the car, no mobile phone to call car mechanic? May one say that it is not possible to replace the wheel without jack? No, because if the question had been posed in other way, like how it is possible to lift car's side without jack, the possible solutions could be:

1. to approach to some ditch with a pierced wheel so as to put it in the air;

1. to pick up car's side with stick or log;

2. to inflate the remaining 3 tires to the uttermost.

Situation No.2. Some engineers had been given the task to create a soundless firearm. A shot, from acoustic point of view is a sound way with a particular "pressure and frequency". (15, 243) Human's ear does not hear the whole sound spectrum, but only a particular diapason from it. The right question for engineers would be: how to create the firearm which shooting's sound will be out of human perception spectrum? The correct answer to the correctly posed question would be "nozzle". (29, 356) Changing its diameter one will be able to change sound wave's parameters considerably. Evidently there may be other technical solutions reducing the sound: barrel's metal, gunpowder's chemical composition, "subsonic ammunition". (25, 17)

Situation No.3. It is known that during the Second World War pontoon bridges over rivers had been destroyed massively by "bombers" (2, 61) because they were seen from air easily. In order to hide them some innovation must have been invented. The right question here is: how to make a pontoon bridge invisible for enemy aircrafts` crew? The right answer here is to submerge it under the water to the depth of approximately 1 meter.* In this case the bridge is submerged and barely seen from the air and at the same time military transport could drive on it. No doubt that other additional means how to camouflage the bridge exist: color, camouflage, but they play supportive role here.

* Once read from memoirs of WW2 participant.

If smart question approach may be applied in engineering, then it could be effectively implemented in immigration service work as well. It is reasonable to include teaching of smart question method into officials` training program concretely as "a repeatable process". (53, 12)

CHAPTER 2

Contemporary people in the civilized world, especially the young ones, may justly be defined as "net generation." (40, 5) This metaphor is not an exaggeration since one can easily notice that generally we "write" more messages than letters, read or better to say skim more announcements, advertisements than we read literature, pay more by credit card than by cash. Taking into account the tendency to digitalize everything that is electronically nonnumeric, paper money will be eventually replaced by e-money. Though this implementation process is not going on smoothly due to the considerable concerns "about the impact of e-money on tax collection and criminal activity" (24, 5) but nevertheless it is developing.

One example of some increasing digitalization that is a sad fact that those now who write more than others are generally pupils "at schools." (31, 117) The conveniences brought by penetrating digitalization process seem to be the progress itself, but nevertheless they possess not only advantages, but hide disadvantages as well. As one of them is inclusive, general regress of reading skills among modern humans which as a consequence may eventually lead to readers` complains that "I can not understand" what here is written. (52, 55) Reading, in its turn, is in direct relationship with writing because "reading skills influence writing skills." (64, 216) Reading ability most often precedes writing and there exist strong reading-writing link because "instructions in reading can be effective in improving writing" (7, 89) and generally speaking one may conclude that the worse one reads the worse one writes.

Comparative irrelevance to read and write will cause far-reaching consequences not only in teaching methodology, but in paperwork as well. General decrease in writing skills and as the consequence substitution of handwriting with taping may also deprive investigators of some vital evidences because even handwriting's pressure may unravel its author's "firmness, vitality, capability to work, endurance." (21, 15) Nevertheless one has to admit that exhausting evidences from handwriting may be multiply compensated by the ones from e-mails, social networks.

The research conducted in the USA showed that in "1960 young men read newspapers as much as their fathers, grandfathers but in 2000 young men aged 18-29 read half of the amount read by their parents." (10, 177) And the less one reads the less one is able to read which manifests itself in inability to "decode words, comprehend text, activate personal knowledge during reading," (30, 340) Unfortunately reading is not "inherited" ability (60, 205), and it is not only spelling of words, but also drawing comparisons, conclusions and "understanding" meaning of the text. (58, 23) Here one can draw very important conclusion that reading is not simply the ability to spell words, but more complicated one: comparing facts, drawing conclusions. Even if contemporary people read something, their reading materials consist mainly of announcements, advertisements and operating instructions. Such texts are exceptionally "interactive" containing a lot of "media forms." (65, 60) The above-mentioned interactive insertions are called adaptations which usually manifest themselves in the form of drawings, animation and video. The adopted text, besides its evident advantages of being easily and quickly comprehended by contemporary TV and net-generation, conceals an inevitable disadvantage - atrophy of reading skills. One should remember that original legal text, like law, decree or regulation does not contain any of the above-mentioned adaptations and each official must be able to read it because otherwise being misunderstood it may cause serious consequences. If a person does not read his or her reading skills will diminish gradually because "good readers read considerably more than poor readers both in and out of school,"(17, 49). Legal texts intentionally composed to differ from other ones particularly with terminology, if-then links therefore their "textuality seems to be pragmatically uninteresting" for contemporary readers (46, 250)

If a reader is indeed able to read, he can perform it in two different ways: a) scanning b) skimming. Skimming is a fast reading when a reader "skims" the text in order to get main idea and scanning on the contrary – searching for "particular" facts or details. (55, 51) Application of one or another method depends on reader's aim, so if the official is already acquainted with the text but he wants to elaborate details- he uses scanning, and otherwise if there is new instruction he initially uses skimming to get meaning. Service instruction or law being misread and misunderstood by an official may cause various drastic consequences. The impact produced will depend on official's occupation, rank etc but nevertheless there exist some approaches which greatly improve text understanding: a) "reading aloud" (58, 180) b) after-reading exercises which include asking three "w" questions: "who? when? where"? (68, 358) Each reader may ask these questions to himself to comprehend text better.

Legal texts are also notable for their "substantiality" and "neutrality" of emotions. (71, 51) „Distinction between facts and events" determines a specific composition of legal text. (46, 248) Legal language may be embarrassing for those who must implement it in practice including policemen, border guards because not all of them will be able to comprehend its meaning. To prove the latter statement let us read a sentence from immigration law: *"country of residence – the country of citizenship of a foreigner ‚ the foreigner's previous country of permanent place of residence"*. (39) First, one may wonder how much time means "permanent": one year, ten years? Second, what is the meaning of comma in this sentence? Third, what is the country of residence if for example a Syrian citizen has been living permanently in Turkey? According to the formal logic comma could mean both conjunctions "and", "or". If comma means "or" then "or", in its turn, „can be inclusive or exclusive". (1, 121) Inclusive means that the sentence is truth when "one or both" (1, 121) component parts of the sentence divided by "or" are truth. Let us interpret the sentence inclusively, *country of residence is- the country of citizenship of a foreigner or previous country of permanent place of residence or both country of citizenship and previous country of permanent place of residence.*

Exclusive means that the sentence is false when its "disjuncts are *both* truth". (1, 121) So, *country of residence is - the country of citizenship or previous country of permanent place of residence but not both at the same time.*

Taking into account, the difficulties interpreting a text, especially the legal one, legislators should firstly solve one vital problem before elaborating laws, service instructions: how to get text more comprehensible for a contemporary reader? There could be two solutions: 1) to teach reading techniques 2) to adapt text according to readers' ability. If the first solution requires elaboration and an organization of reading improvement courses that are directly-proportionally connected with time, money, then the second one requires making instructions more comprehensible for contemporary readers. A text redesigned with the purpose to be more understandable for readers is called adaptive, like for example a text in simple English. The process of textual adaptation may include substitution with synonyms, simplification of grammar with the aim of creating a final product-the summary containing only vital information. Reader himself may perform the task of textual adaptation in order to aggregate information, but he should be prepared for it because it „is not an easy task because the reader is required to complete multiple steps to create a successful product." (51, 205) Nowadays textual adaptation may be conveniently discharged applying modern technical achievements because they provide"many choices available on desktop computers, tablets, mobile phones." (62, 117)

CHAPTER 3

It is he or it is not he? That's the main question not only for a granny with huge spectacles impatiently watching out for her grandchildren out of her window, but in the highest degree it is the question for policemen, investigators, border guards etc. For these categories of servicemen the right answer to this question is of high importance. For example, a policeman has stopped some man having no documents with him; the man is reluctant to cooperate with the policeman and is very similar to the wanted one whose photo is hanging on the call board of his police office. Who is he then? Now the policeman has only two possibilities: to let him go or to detain him on the basis to check his identity. For policeman every choice contains risks and mistakes consequently:

1) if I release him and he is wanted? (Mistake- to release the criminal)

2) if I detain him, but he is "clear"? (Mistake- to detain the innocent)

The first mistake, let us call it "the first class of mistakes" (72, 97) happened because policeman thought that criminal's photo and his appearance were too different and the man in front of him and the one on the picture were different ones. The second mistake, let us call it "the second class of mistakes" (72, 98) happened because policeman thought that criminal's photo and person's appearance were too similar and the man in front of him and the one on the picture was the same person. Both "kinds of mistakes are unwanted for society" (72, 98), but they do happen. Here, should be mentioned that facial recognition has not been the only way of identification since there are applied both manual and automatic checks of passports, ID cards in checks, but nevertheless initial positive facial recognition may lead to person's detention. Anyway facial recognition may serve as a proof in some cases, though its role can not be decisive in final conviction. Identification mistakes may happen not only in face recognition system, but further in investigation and court proceedings, for example the USA alone "350 defendants had been wrongfully convicted in capital cases in the period from 1900 to 1985". (50, 9) Evidently even after the year 1985 this grim destiny is still taking its toll not only in the States, but worldwide.

But let us return to identification mistakes, if they are inevitable indeed then how can one decrease their number and consequences caused by them? First of all, let us discern which of these two kinds of mistakes leads to more drastic consequences. The answer is that the second kind of mistake is greater than the first one. It is easy to compare, if we evaluate "the damage from releasing the criminal "with the number **A**" (72, 98), then the damage from detaining the innocent person "with the number **B**". (72, 98) In this case we can see that the first kind of mistakes "leads to the damage **A**, but the second- to the damage **A+B**". It is difficult to say in which units it is possible to evaluate both damages, but here the principal thing is to "determine which damage is higher and this can be done with formula:

"$q = \dfrac{A+B}{B}$ "(72, 98)

"If A=B" (72, 98) it means that the damage from detaining the innocent is two times higher. Further in this chapter the author will analyse possible remote identification process in the cases when a suspect refuses to cooperate and when a discrete observation is applicable. Successful process of remote facial identification may sound unachievable, but nevertheless street camera continuously filming people and computer software processing and comparing images is the fact. Its machinery is the following: if the software finds sufficient facial similarity it informs a policeman on duty instantly. After having been informed, a policeman on duty moves to the spot for the further investigation. Here, the main challenge is to find out exact number of differences or similarities which are enough to consider a person filmed to be unwanted or wanted. How to solve that problem?

Let us define the amount of difference with "some number Q." (72, 98) If this number is too high then two facial images seem different, if it is too low they seem similar. Ultimately, "if there were not any interference" (72, 99) like person's age-related changes, clothes, weather, facial gestures... the problem would be solved very simply "if Q=0 faces are identical, if Q > 0 faces are different". (72, 99)   But the interference...they change everything, due to them it may be that "Q=0 but faces are different, Q > 0 faces are similar". (72, 99) The problem is how it is possible to discern images at all? The answer is – to apply the "decisive rule". (72, 99) This rule sounds as follows: "if a number of differences Q is higher than some number r then the faces are different" (72, 99) and the suspect is "clear", but "if Q is lower than number r the faces are considered identical" (72, 99) and a person is the suspect. Identification's subsequent failures and successes will depend on this number r because if "it is = 0 or is too low" (72, 99) then an investigator, according to the decisive rule will not detain the innocent and the offender will escape as well. Here an investigator commits the first class of mistake (A-to loose the offender). Otherwise, "if the r number is too high the suspect will be detained but the innocent will be detained as well." (72, 99) Here the second class of mistake may be committed (B-to detain the innocent) and this failure causes damage A+B (the offender is released but the innocent) In order to minimize risks of both mistakes the r number must be "averaged out" (72,99) in other words the "golden mean" must be found.

Generally speaking, risk appearance is expressed with the formula "potential loss x probability of occurrence". (45, 19) *"Expertise risk function* defines the average r number with the formula $R = A \times p_1 + (A + B) \times p_2$" (72, 99) where A and B, as it was written before, are damages of releasing an offender and detaining an innocent, p_1 - offender acquittal's probability or the degree of "conviction that the first kind of mistakes will occur" (72, 99) and p_2 - innocent detention probability or the degree of "conviction that the second kind of mistakes will occur". (72,99) The values p_1 and p_2 depend on r value. (See the next figure) Let us summarize, if $r =$ is too low or equal 0, then the probability that the first class of mistakes will occur is 100% $p_1=1$, if r is too high or equal 1 then the probability that the second class of mistakes will occur is 100% $p_2 = 1$.

Figure No.3.1. Probabilities p_1 and p_2 and their dependence on r value (72,100)

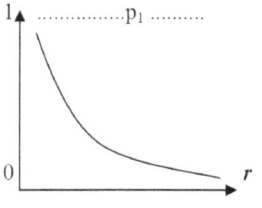 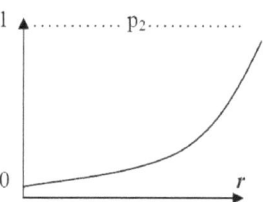

0-1-probability (from 0 to 100 %)

r- value

p_1- offender acquittal's probability

p_2- innocent detention probability

Let us now put drawing's No.1 values in formula $R = A * p_1 + (A + B)* p_2$ so that we can get investigation risk's dependence on r value. This dependence is visualized in the next figure.

Figure No.3.2. Investigation risk's dependence on r value (72, 100)

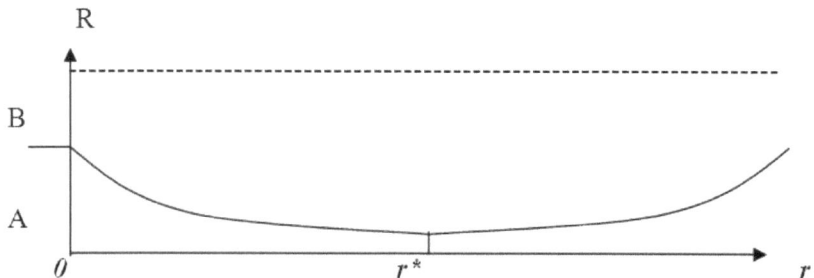

R- risk

A- offender acquittal's risk

B- innocent detention probability risk

r- value

r^*- the best value

From this drawing, one can discern that minimal identification risk is r^*. In order to minimize investigation mistakes and their damages an investigator must choose r^* value.

The present paragraph showed possible mathematical solutions of remote face identification, using surveillance cameras placed almost at every street of modern city. In the relevant survey the border guards have been asked to find r^* value. The survey has been conducted to define how similar suspected person's face must be in comparison with criminal's image in order to consider them identical. In this survey it is to find value r^*.

- 0% means that the faces are completely different, 50 % the faces are partly different 100 % the faces are identical

Respondents: 10 borderguards	Average value r* in percents 78 %

the table designed by the author

From the respondents' point of view if r^* or the similarity degree between a suspect and an image is more than 78% there is reason to believe that they are identical and vice versa.   Contemporary precise face recognition methods are based on biometrical techniques because „face is captured using a scanner" and the data are obtainable from "2 D, 3 D, infra red scanners" (22, 183) Apart from facial recognition from distance, biometrical one is more fragile and demanding, but these inconveniences are fully compensated with its comparative accuracy. Logical question may arise whether it is possible to perform a biometrical check from distance "in unconstrained environments with uncooperative subjects"? (6, 182) Although some authors claim that remote identification may be considered biometric as well because unique biometric material like iris image can be obtainable and processable even from a subject "walking through the hallway" (48, 6) that is from far distance, but nevertheless the author of the paper wants to mark the inevitable interferences like distance, weather, illumination, person's aging, etc which will ultimately degrade accuracy of remote identification. Considering these facts, one may conclude the farther from camera or scanner is a person, the worse is identification degree.

Picture No.1. (48, 53)

Combined Face and Iris Recognition System (CFAIRS) built by Honeywell for face and iris acquisition and recognition at ranges from 1.5 to beyond 4 m. The device stands a bit less than 2 m high. Picture courtesy of Rand Whillock of Honeywell

SUBCHAPTER 3. 1

Inversely proportional correspondence between distance and quality of identification will influence the choice, implementation and installation of identification system. However, here one should mention another extreme when the image of a person standing too near or in immediate proximity of camera or scanner will be blurred. Having analysed and compared different scientific studies the author may conclude that facial recognition systems generally underperform in comparison with id systems comparing man's biometric data such as fingerprints, voice, DNA, etc. These data being inserted and analysed in biometric software "gain nearly 100- percent authentication rates." (23, 68)   But nevertheless both systems may have one common feature- this is the r^* value approach or speaking in mathematical language - algorithm. The general idea of this approach, as it has been mentioned in the previous chapter, is to find balance between two main mistakes occurring in identification systems: false acceptance/ wrong consent.

Regardless of identification system's parameters, application each has its own authentication rate and this rate may depend on many factors like: technical ones (camera, computer, processing program), external ones (weather, air pollution, electromagnetic interference). Facial recognition from distance is more vulnerable to the external interferences than the biometrical system. The latter is usually installed in airports, offices and requires person's consent to the procedures. But at the same time remote identification's *main* advantage – discrete surveillance and comparison of data "has gained considerable traction" (6, 182) recently.

In the table below the author will try to postulate the effectiveness of both face recognition system from distance and biometrical one. Of course there are being implemented various facial, biometrical systems possessing distinct parameters, produced in Europe, in the USA, but let us at least extract average, general differences.

Table No.3.1.1. Possible identification degree

Face recognition system-FRS	**Biometric ID system-BIS** (eyes iris, fingerprints and etc.)
Less than 100 % but more than 50 % * if its identification degree was not more that 50% the system would be ineffective	Nearly. 100 % (56, 68)

* the table designed by the author

Nevertheless, let us return to face recognition systems. As it has been written before, identification system's efficiency depends on many circumstances. Experiments on face recognition were conducted in the USA where some hundred subjects' facial images under variable illumination or facial expression were compared. In these experiments (over 100) the best average recognition rate achieved" i.e. correct rejection and identification" was 85,4 %. (34, 106) In other face comparison experiments conducted in "non-intrusive way" subject's distance from face extracting system was of importance. (5, 341) Here recognition system's produced errors were directly proportional to the distance from a target: close distance- 1,43% of errors, medium distance- 18,06% and far distance- 82,57%. (5, 344)

Every system's efficiency is inversely proportional to the mistakes committed. The fewer mistakes are committed the better system performs and vice versa. System's mistake probability may be expressed by standard formula: $P(A)=m/n$, where $P(A)$-the probability of false acceptance and false rejection = cases of false acceptance and rejection / all identification cases. Probability of system mistake varies from 0 to 1, which literally means: 0- will never happen, 1-will happen hundred-presently. In the case of BIS in ideal conditions, the probability of false identification is nearly zero.

34

Returning to our investigator and a "suspected," here the investigator can commit two kinds of mistakes: "detaining an innocent person" and "releasing the guilty one". In identification system's language these mistakes are called consequently: "false acceptance rate-FAR" and "false rejection rate-FRR". (23, 68) The first kind of mistake, namely false acceptance, happens when the system falsely announces sufficient similarity between the data inserted into the system and the data which is already in the system's database. The second kind of mistake, namely false rejection, happens when the system falsely announces sufficient differences between the data inserted into the system and the data which is already in the system's database. Nevertheless, BIS is more reliable and precise one in comparison with FRS.

Researches show that *iris* and *fingerprints*, being of course biometrical material, are the most reliable sources for identification. (see the table below)

Table No. 3.1.2. **Error rates for BIS** (41, 450)

Selected Technology Error Rates

Biometric	Face	Finger	Iris
FTE % (Failure to enroll)	n/a	4	7
FNMR % rejection rates	4	2.5	6
FMR1 % verification match error rate	10	<0.01	<0.001
FMR2 % identification error rates for dB size > 1 m	40	0.1	N/A
FMR3 % screening match error rate for dB sizes = 500	12	<1	N/A

Note: Typical biometric accuracy performance numbers reported in large third-party tests. FNMR (also ERR) and FMR (also FAR). N/A is nonavailable data.

Other researches on reliability of BIS had been performed in the UK in National Physical Laboratory and they are following:

Figure 3.1. **Error rates for BIS** (36, 465)

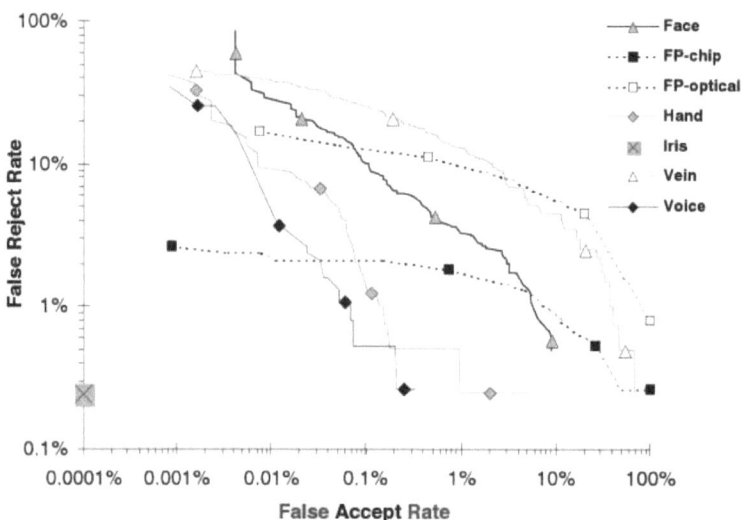

Here, each square or triangle represents a particular test performed and balances between FAR and FRR. One may truly conclude that biometric identification system is quite reliable and precise but comparatively expensive, since processing of DNA makes it exceptionally valuable due to the connection with sensitive issue – "personal freedom". (22, 178)

As it has been written before contemporary young generation in modern world could be justly called the net generation, but if there is the net there must be the "spider" to weave his net. If we continue to explicate this metaphor further, then apart from the "spider" holding strings and managing the net there must be "pray" which will be caught in it. Contemporary modern citizen almost fully depends on his credit card since without electronic money he will fail or have considerable difficulties to pay mortgage, to buy food, medicine; all his transactions with credit card are transparent. At the end it may happen that some day the civilized world will become electronic concentration camp where the authorities as the principal possessor of personal data will draw certain conclusions from records including "school, college, medical, employment, credit history"? (61, 9)

Here, each square or triangle represents a particular test performed and balances between FAR and FRR. One may truly conclude that biometric identification system is quite reliable and precise but comparatively expensive, since processing of DNA makes it exceptionally valuable due to the connection with sensitive issue – "personal freedom." (22, 178)

As it has been written before contemporary young generation in contemporary world could be justly called the net generation, but if there is the net there must be the "spider" to weave his net. If we continue to explicate this metaphor further, then apart from the "spider" holding strings and managing the net there must be "prey" which will be caught in it. Contemporary modern citizen almost fully depends on his credit card since without electronic money he will fail or have considerable difficulties paying mortgage, to bye food, medicine; all his transactions with credit card are transparent. At the end it may happen that someday the civilized world will become electronic concentration camp where the authorities as the principal possessor of personal data will draw certain conclusions from records including "school, college, medical, employment, credit history"? (61, 9)

Nevertheless, let us return to the systems, as it has been mentioned before both FRS and BIS perform identification with errors, but BIS works almost without them, especially when some biometrical data is processed for one check.

And what about using both FRS and BIS simultaneously? For example, some person was walking on the street and had been captured on a surveillance camera and then his facial image was automatically compared in FRS as a result FRS reported authentication. Then, the same person's face had been compared in BIS with the same result. Let's imagine that in this situation both FRS and BIS made the error is called –false acceptance, which means that an innocent person had been considered the suspect. According to the multiplication of probability such scenario can happen with possibility approximately 0,05 %, which means that in theory, approximately one of 2000 checked by both systems will be that "the innocent" person whom the systems would consider guiltily. (see the table below)

Table No. 3.1.3. **Systems' error possibility in % comparing** *faces*

FRS	FRS error possibility (for example 5 %)	BIS (for example 1 %)	BIS error possibility	The possibility that both FRS and BIS will error simultaneously
To detain an innocent person	0,05 (or 5 %)	False acceptance (to detain an innocent person)	0.01(1 %)	0,05*0,01 =0,0005 (0,05%)

* the table designed by the author

Table No. 3.1.4. **Occurrence of false acceptance comparing face, fingerprints, iris in diverse conditions** (73)

Biometry	False acceptance	Persons	Commentary
Face	1 %	37437	Different light indoor/outdoor
Fingerprints	1 %	25000	The USA government data
Iris	0.94 %	1224	Indoor environment

In table 3.1.3 only faces had been compared that is why the comparison of other biometrical data like iris, fingerprints would greatly decrease possibility of errors. Iris is our unique feature and the "chance of two irises being identical is estimated at 1 in 10 [78] (22, 189) For example if we include in comparison not only face, but iris and fingerprints as well, in this case only approximately one of 21276595 checked people will be falsely accepted an innocent man. (see the table below) For certain, the insertion of iris and fingerprints in the list of comparison decreases wrong identification possibility up to 10 000 times. However, unfortunately such complex check will take more time and identification procedure will loose its discreetness.

In the following example the two systems had been cooperating in sequence: 1) FRS-performed surveillance, preliminary identification 2) BIS- did final identification.

Table No. 3.1.5. **Systems' error probability %, comparing face, fingerprints and iris.**

FRS	FRS error possibility (for example 5 %)	BIS (face, fingerprints and iris data taken from the table No.3.1.4.)	The possibility of simultaneous face, fingerprints and iris data to be wrongly consented	The possibility that both FRS and BIS will error simultaneously
False acceptance	0,05 (or 5 %)	False acceptance	0,01*0,01*0,0094 =0,00000094	0,05*0,00000094 =0,000000047 (0,0000047%)

* *the table designed by the author*

If both systems are operating the investigator has to take decision according to the systems' results and here the "last word" belongs to BIS as being much more precise. At the same time, the investigator has the rights not to agree with systems results if he is certain that the error had occurred. In the following figure one can see investigator's possible actions if he does not agree with the system.

Figure No. 3.1.2. **Possible actions having received BIS hit „ identified or wanted"**

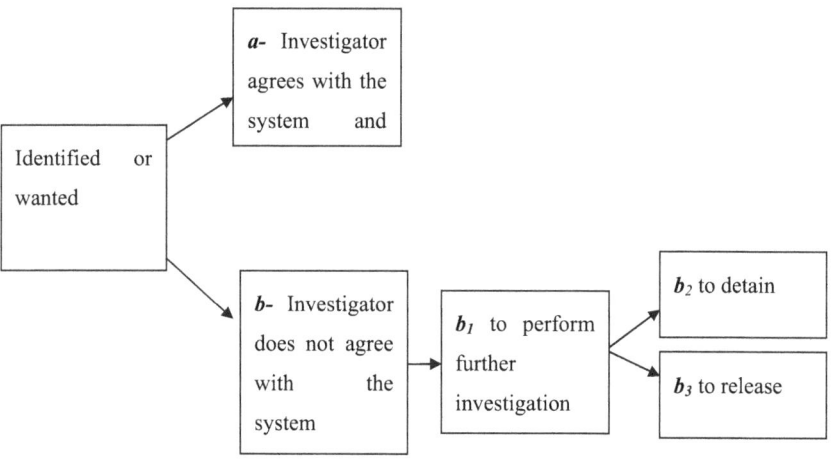

a, b, b₁, b₂ b₃-decisions taken by investigator

* the figure designed by the author

Despite investigator's supreme right to ignore system's hits and considering BIS micro possibility of error he nevertheless, will usually obey the system and take decision *a.* Finally it is hard to imagine the situation when an investigator should not agree with BIS, if only the person who is being checked is his close relative or friend above suspicion.

SUBCHAPTER 3.1.1

Comparing both systems one can discern their advantages and disadvantages. For example:

FRS advantages:

a) the suspected may not know that he is being filmed and his data is being processed;

b) FRS is much cheaper than BIS; (see the next table)

c) FRS data is acquirable in almost every modern city; (surveillance cameras considerably prevail over biometrical data scanners)

d) Contains considerably less size of data than BIS (templates of biometric data: iris, face may have the size up to 300 MB). (47, 317)

e)

FRS disadvantages:

a) Has lower identification rate that BIS.

Table No. 3.1.1.1. Necessary equipment for both systems

Face Identification System- FRS	Biometrical Identification System- BIS (iris, fingerprints)
1. Face shooting devices (surveillance cameras, cameras) 2. Image processing (extraction) program	1. Scanner for iris 2. Scanner for fingerprints 3. DNA expertise 4. Signature comparison 5. Lighting

* the table designed by the author

The summary of this chapter can be the following- both systems are particularly accurate when being used simultaneously. For example, the suspect has been filmed walking on the street, then FRS automatically compares face footage gives a preliminary answer whether the suspect is wanted or not wanted. If FRS answer is "wanted" the investigator makes the decision to detain the suspect and check his data in BIS. And otherwise, if FRS answer is "not wanted" the investigator may not detain the person. Simultaneous usage of both systems creates the particular sequence of actions. In this case, FRS is like a traffic light, which gives a green signal – the person is "wanted" or red one- "not wanted" and BIS completes person's final identification.

Now let us follow investigator's logic after having received hit "wanted" from FRS. Having received the hit "wanted" the investigator receives additional information from the system- wanted for what? Let us imagine that in this case the reason for search is foreigner's outstanding "departure order" meaning that the suspect was supposed to leave the country in time, but he had not and was residing in the country illegally. The investigator has only two decisions to take: to detain or not to detain. The most expected decision would be, of course to detain. Let us imagine that in this case the suspect is "wanted" because his face correlation or similarity degree to the "wanted "person from FRS database is approximately 70%. That means if correlation was less that 70% FRS would answer "not wanted." Here comes vital conclusion that system's answer depends on this correlation degree or threshold. (the above mention r-number) But how to determine the number of threshold separating hits "wanted" and "not wanted"? Programmers understand that if a number of the threshold is too low that could mean that the investigator will depart for suspect detention more frequently and subsequently the risk to detain an innocent man will increase. And otherwise if the threshold is too high, for example more than 90%, the investigator will detain suspects less often, but at the same it increases the risk to release or not to notice the "wanted" one because of the latter one whose correlation degree is less than 90% will escape. That is why it is important to find that "the golden mean" or consequently r or r^* number.

CHAPTER 4

The proverb says that it is better one time to have a look at something than to hear about it a hundred times. And that is quite true since "graphical information is more expressive than textual one" (54, 621) since "graphical information is stored in memory better than text." (54, 621) Realizing this feature of our psyche, designers create contemporary advertisements with domination of graphical and sound elements over textual ones. One of the ways in which to optimize or summarize necessary text is morphological analysis. Morphological analysis is a graphical one, and it has been invented and developed by Swiss scientist Fritz Zwicky. Originally, Greek word "*morphe*" means the teaching of "shape" (56, 198) describing its structure, components and their interaction. In simple words this is an absolute *division* of an object.

Morphological analysis can be applied in many scientific branches, for example in "medicine" (components: body, its parts), in "sociology" (components: organization, chief...). (59, 3) In order to reveal composition of the whole and the parts, Zwicky had invented the schedule which was later named nominally "Zwicky box". The meaning of his box is in arrangement of different components in "n-dimensional matrix". (59, 3) The aim of the analysis of the box is to find out "different and single alternatives." (59, 3) Classical example of Zwicky box is the 3-dimentional cube consisting of 75 various cells. (see the next picture). For example, there is necessary to find out all possible objects in the box containing three dimensions: "size, quality, color" (12, 1). Each dimension contains its own characteristics, for example the dimension *color* may contain characteristics or colors: red, green, blue, yellow, brown, the dimension *quality*: smooth, irregular, hard, meek, half irregular, *size*: huge, middle, small. Subsequently there are "5 x 5 x 3 = 75" different cells or objects (12, 1).

Figure 4.1. 3-dimensional " Zwicky box" (12, 1)

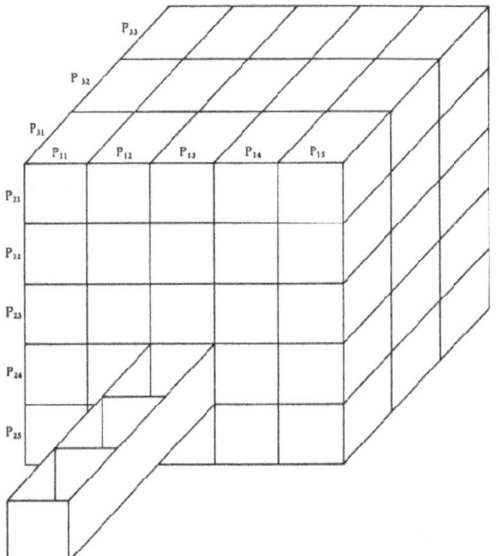

P-dimension

P_{11} to P_{15}-*color* dimension (P_{11}-red color, P_{12}-green, P_{13}-blue, P_{14}-yellow, P_{15}-brown);

P_{21} to P_{25}- *quality* dimension (P_{21}-smooth, P_{22}-irregular, P_{23}-hard, P_{24}-meek, P_{25}- half irregular);

P_{31} to P_{33}- *size* dimension (P_{31}-huge, P_{32}-middle, P_{33}-small);

P_{21}, P_{11}, P_{31}-name of the cell „smooth, red, huge".

Each cell contains three characteristics, for example: smooth, red, huge which are subsequently P_{21}, P_{11}, P_{31}. Each cell is always unique because it contains at least one different parameter in comparison with any other cell. (see the next drawing) As it was written above, morphological analysis is widely used by engineers, designers in order to "account an array of possibilities that are too extensive for the mind to track". (3, 91) For

44

example, even from three dimensions containing: color (5 colors), quality-5, size-3 a furniture or car designer is able to extract 75 different seats.

Figure No.4.2. **Two adjacent cells**

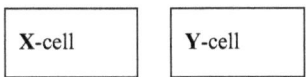

Cell x contains characteristics: (P_{21}, P_{11}, P_{31}) cell y contains characteristics (P_{21}, P_{12}, P_{31});

Cell x is (smooth, red, huge), cell y is (smooth, green, huge).

* the figure designed by the author

Having found all possible variations, Zwicky suggested that all of them should be analysed in order to extract the "best" ones. (59, 5) Approximately until 1995 the job of extraction all possible variation from the data given was on "scientists` shoulders" but now contemporary computer software performs this action quickly and accurately. (63, 8)

One should note, that the above described three dimensional Zwicky box is a representative sample because boxes containing hundreds, thousands dimensions exist. For example, in order to "forecast one type of rocket engine" there is necessary to build "eleven axes with 36,864 combinations". (28, 62) For certain, that no human can extract and analyse 36,864 variations as rapidly and fundamentally as a software.

Before completing morphological analysis, one needs to know an optimal sequence of actions. In simple words an analyst should know where to begin? This is called hierarchy of actions. Hierarchy is "the total construction of system's levels" (8, 13) For example, a car designer will surely start designing the car with the most important dimensions like: P w- car wheels, P e- engine, P b- body metal and it is unlikely that he will begin designing with P c- color of chairs. And it appears from this that morphological analysis main disadvantage is possible loss of dimensions which may cause the further exclusion of associated dimensions and their parameters. The loss of dimensions and parameters included in them may be both inessential like (P c- color of chairs) and essential (P em- metal of engine).

SUBCHAPTER 4.1

During the shift or patrol a policeman may take various decisions of various complexities in tight time. How to accelerate decision taking process and at the same time not to deteriorate, but on the contrary to improve its quality? The hypothesis may be that with Zwicky box it could be possible to achieve both these parameters. For example, one can design the 2-dimentional table which may contain possible actions applied to the administrative violators. (see the next table) The table below reflects accepted, possible actions detaining a foreigner without any personal documents.

Table No. 4.1.1. **A foreigner with or without travel documents.**

| | P(s) –status | | | |
	3-rd country national having passport or other ID	**3-rd country national having no passport or other ID**	**EU citizen**	**Asylum seeker**
P(v)-violation **Residing without residence permit**	1.to detain; 2. explain rights and duties; 3.take explanation; 4.draw up protocol; 5 release or detain…	1.to detain; 2. explain rights and duties; 3.take explanation; 4.draw up protocol; 5 move to immigration centre…	1.to detain; 2. explain rights and duties; 3.take explanation; 4.draw up protocol; 5 release.	no residence permit required
Residing without visa	1.to detain; 2. explain rights and duties; 3.take explanation; 4.draw up protocol; 5 release or detain…	1.to detain; 2. explain rights and duties; 3.take explanation; 4.draw up protocol; 5 move to immigration centre…	no visa required	no visa required
Delay in registration of residence permit	1.to detain; 2. explain rights and duties; 3.take explanation; 4.draw up protocol; 5 release…	1.to detain; 2. explain rights and duties; 3.take explanation; 4.draw up protocol; 5 move to immigration centre…	1.to detain; 2. explain rights and duties; 3.take explanation; 4.draw up protocol; 5 release.	no registration required

the table designed by the author

Such table is the summary of several laws, operating instructions and it is convenient and portable visual summary. Due to the lack of space on the paper, this table does not represent *all* possible dimensions and characteristics. For example, the dimension P (s) – person status could be further enriched with statuses like:

1. an asylum seeker in other EU Member State;

2. an asylum seeker in the third country;

1. an asylum who had been granted asylum status in this country;

2. an asylum who had been granted asylum status in EU Member State;

3. an asylum who had been granted asylum status in the third country;

4. person having an alternative status;

5. ...

In its turn each of them can be divided into other sub statuses:

1.   **an asylum seeker in other Member State**:

1.1   an asylum seeker in other Member State holder of diplomatic passport;

1.2.   an asylum seeker in other Member State holder of ordinary passport;

1.3.   an asylum seeker in other Member State holder of official passport;

1.4.   an asylum seeker in other Member State holder of emergency passport.

Policeman's action will differ depending on the person's status; presumably there should be difference between treating asylum seeker-holder of diplomatic passport and the one having an ordinary passport. Due to the diplomatic immunity diplomats can not be "arrested or detained" while asylum seekers having no immunity may be subjected to detention. (27, 166) The same way the dimension P (v) –violation can be also enriched with other characteristics, sub characteristics like articles from administrative, criminal, international laws. Having designed a complete two-dimensional table there would appear extensional, clumsy, paper table in the end. Complete paper tables may not be handy and will fail to fit into A4 paper format due to the huge amount of information on little space.

Therefore, there appears the need to replace multidimensional, paper tables with "multidimensional matrix" and it can be successfully completed by relevant software programs. (20, 1) There exists a lot of software for both morphological analysis and decision tree but the commonest is "SAS Enterprise Miner" (37). This software contains a lot of functions including designing decision trees of various categories, objects, values.

For example, if it is necessary to extract all acceptable and prohibited actions in the situation where an official must check foreigners' identity, morphological analysis may be applied. In this case following categories or dimensions may be considered: **S**-person status- **4** statuses, **V**- violation articles-**6** articles, **E**-explanations-**3** forms, **P**-protocols-**3** protocol forms, **R**-reporting-to report **5** recipients, **DP**-detention palces-**3** places and **DT**-detention terms-**4** possible detention terms. The total amount of various combinations here will be 4 x 6 x 5 x 3 x 3 x 3 x 4 = 12960! And all combinations will look like:

Table No.4.1.2. **Sequential chain of actions in the case of violation.**

Sequence number	S	V	E	P	R	DP	DT
1.	3-rd country national	Residing without visa	Explanation form No.1	Protocol form No.1	To report a senior officer	Temporary detention room	Up to 3 hours
2.	3-rd country national	Residing without visa	Explanation form No.1	Protocol form No.1	To report a senior officer	Temporary detention room	Up to 10 days
3.	3-rd country national	Residing without visa	Explanation form No.1	Protocol form No.1	To report a senior officer	Temporary detention room	Up to 2 months
...12960	...	...	...	...	...	...	...

the table designed by the author

If we encode the content of the table it will look like:

Table No.4.1.3. **Sequential, encoded chain of actions in the case of violation.**

Sequence number	S	V	E	P	R	DP	DT	Action's code
1.	S	V	E	P	R	DP	DT	SVEPRDPDT
2.	S	V	E	P	R	DP	DT 2	SVEPRDPDT2
3.	S	V	E	P	R	DP	DT 3	SVEPRDPDT3
...12960	...	...	...	...	...	...	...	

* the table designed by the author

Here S is the 3-rd country national; V- residing without visa; E-explanation form No.1; P- protocol form No.1; R- to inform a senior officer; DP- temporary detention room; DT-to detent up to 3 hours; DT 2 -to detent up to 10 days, DT 3 to detent up to 2 months. For every new status, violation, etc a sequence number will be given. For example: DT, DT 2, DT 3; S, S 2, S 3...

The above designed extensive table proves that it is impossible to represent all possible combinations on the paper. To make the table more efficient its categories can be placed sequentially. In other words, policeman meets a person, having checked his passport he finds out that the person is the foreigner residing without visa than he takes explanation and writes protocol, informs senior officer, brings violator to the detention room where the detainee is in cell up to three hours. In the table the square DT 3 is marked with red color because according to the Latvian immigration law it is prohibited to detain a foreigner up to 2 months without judge decision.

Upon completing all 12960 combinations many of them will be illegal to implement due to their incompliance with laws, and further they could be marked with red color. Few policemen in the world may know that their "ordinary" actions starting from the check of documents to the final decision may contain more than a thousand variations! But on the other hand they should not keep in mind all possible variations because in a particular situation they act according to service instructions which get within actual law. If policemen should comply with the operating instructions, designers should create them firstly. If an instruction is created by means of morphological analysis, then according to the scientists (44) its development may be divided into the following sequential steps:

1. To outline the problem;
2. To define necessary categories (dimensions– P^n);
3. To include appropriate subcategories (characteristics);
4. To constitute and evaluate all combinations;
5. To choose the best combinations.

If **sequential** table contains dimensions– $P^a P^b P^c$ ...with characteristics $^{a\ b\ c\cdots}$ included, the total amount of combinations can be found by formula: a x b x c....

It is interesting and may be even urgent to develop morphological tables to extract all combinations since the final product of analysis represents all possible variations depending on the data input. Although it may take a lot of time and effort, nevertheless, the productivity of table compensates these expenses. (see the next table) As it was written before morphological analysis is the universal one and can be applied to not only in engineering, but even in medicine to treat blood diseases and create "morphological analysis of the blood cells" (9, 547), in genetics- to "distinguish animal species` relativity degree" (69, 338), but in lawmaking as well.

Table No. 4.1.4. **All possible combinations depending on the number of dimensions and their objects. (if principle of sequence is necessary)**

Dimensions P number	All possible combinations if there are three 3 characteristics in each dimension
2	9
3	27
4	81
5	243
6	729

* the table designed by the author

The operating principle of morphological analysis may be represented not only in the form of a table, but in any other one, for example in the shape of circle. (see the next drawing) Circularity is appropriate when P dimension contains hundreds, thousands characteristics. In this case the circle's content can be distinguished and read by computer software.

Figure No. 4.1.1. **Morphological analysis in the form of circle**

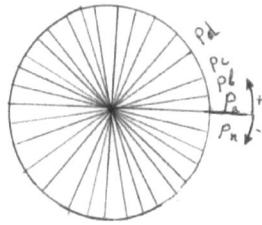

P$_a$, P$_b$... sequence of dimensions.

P (a, b, c, d,... n) dimensions.

* the figure designed by the author

Conclusions:

Decision tree is graphical summary of text;

Application of decision tree significantly decreases decision taking time;

Morphological analysis reveals all possible combinations from the data given;

Depending on the aim of the designer he can draw morphological table by hand or using software program;

Morphological analysis can be used not only in science, but in lawmaking as well;

The application of decision tree or morphological analysis table, which are summaries of a text, may decrease users' reading ability.

CHAPTER 5

Survey No.1. **Decision taking and its risk.**

Table No.5.1

How much do you miss your job? (minutes)	Number of answers	How many times do you miss your job throughout the year?	Number of answers
5	4	3	2
10	7	4	2
15	4	5	10
20	-	7	1
30	-	-	-
More than 30	-	-	-
Missed minutes (average for each borderguard)	10	Average number of times	4,73

* the table designed by the author

There have been interviewed 15 border gards in this survey. The results of this survey show that border guards usually decide to miss the job for approximately 10 minutes, in other words they balance between to much / in time. The balance is expressed in formula that delay for more than 10 minutes will evidently lead to the unpleasant circumstances for them and delay for less than 10 minutes will less likely lead to the unpleasant circumstances.

Survey No. 2. **Reading materials, quantity and quality**

There have been surveyed 7 border guards with the purpose to define the kind of the text they read and time spent on it.

Table No.5.2. **Reading materials, their quantity and quality**

What and how much do you read?							
kind of literature	**surveyed borderguards read hours /per week**						
	1-st border guard	**2-nd**	**3-rd**	**4-th**	**5-th**	**6-th**	**7-th**
reference materials	*1*	-	-	*1*	*3*	-	*2*
science	-	*2*	*2*	-	-	*3*	-
fiction	*2*	*1*	*1*	*1*	-	-	*1*
technical	*2*	-	-	-	*1*	-	*1*
educational	-	*1*	*1*	-	*1*	-	-
On the average	**5**	**4**	**4**	**2**	**5**	**3**	**4**

* the table designed by the author

Table No.5.3. **Original text or adapted one?**

If you want to find particular information from law, instruction do you use original text or adapted text.	Number of answers
Original text	-
Summaries or other adapted materials	-
Both original text and other adapted materials	15

This survey proves that immigration service officials are reluctant to read. As the consequence their reading abilities degenerate and they tend to create summaries, tables or other adapted materials which are more visual, evident, and laconic than "complicated" text.

Survey No. 3. **Writing or "writing" text**

Here was the aim to define whether border guards write letters or tape them? As it is mentioned in theoretical part of the paper it has been proven that writing and reading are closely and directly connected. The more one writes, the better one reads and consequently the better one reads, the better one understands any text including laws, service instructions.

Table No.5.4. **In which form do you compose letters?**

Do you write letters?	Borderguards` replies								Replies totally
	1-st borderguard	2-nd	3-rd	4-th	5-th	6-th	7-th	8-th	
SMS	1	1	1	1	1	1	1	1	8
E-mail	1	1	1	-	1	-	1	-	5
Letter	1	-	-	-	1	-	1	-	3

*8 borderguards had been surveyed * the table designed by the author

Table No.5.5. **Excessive turns of speeches**

What turns of speeches do you think are excessive in laws, operating instructions?	Replies
Repetitions	4
Incoherent text	4
Abstractions	3
Excessive words	2
Abbreviation	1

*8 borderguards had been surveyed * the table designed by the author

Table No.5.5. **Watching TV**

Name of the official	How many hours per day do you watch TV?
R:	2
V:	0,5
P:	1
A:	1,5
L:	2
J:	2
M:	3
S:	1
	1,68 hours. (approx. 1 h. 40 min.)

*8 borderguards had been surveyed * the table designed by the author

Survey No.4. **Criminal or not criminal?**

The situation posed to the officials in this survey was the following: if the border guards used computer software which could automatically discern faces from surveillance camera with facial photo of violators in the data base then what comparison degree or threshold must be fixed in order to discern faces? The software would compare faces shot from a surveillance camera with the ones from the database. The process of recognition and comparison of faces performs with a particular rate of errors. As a result the software will treat the request in the manner: the person x is similar to the person y from the database with a similarity degree of, for example 90 percent. If your duty had been to react to the software hits and send police patrol to the spot then what similarity degree, in your opinion is sufficient to send the patrol? Here 0% -the faces are different, 50%- partly similar, 100%- identical.

The aim of this survey had been to find out value *r*, in other words comparison degree sufficient, from border guards' point of view, to identify a person. As a result 10 borer guards had been surveyed and the average *r* value was 78%.

10 borderguards	Average *r** value - 78%.

* the table designed by the author

Survey No.5. **The State border guard and his duties.**

In this survey 5 border guards have been inquired on their duties. The *aim* of this survey has been to find out all possible duties for which an ordinary policeman is responsible. As one can see from the chart below an average immigration service official surveyed, apart from his direct responsibilities may be a driver, an escort member, an interpreter and therefore he is responsible for car, driving safety, escort rules… Such professional diversity possesses its advantages and disadvantages. From one hand it may lead to high risks to get in a car accident, to mistranslate etc if an official has a lot of different duties, but on the other hand he has chances to become a sort of a "universal soldier" or in managerial language speaking a generalist capable of doing various jobs. In contradiction to "generalist" there may work subject matter officials whose duties are strictly defined: only escort, only driver, only clerk, only translator.

Table No.5.6.

Position	I work as ...x-yes				
-	Driver	Interpreter	State borerguard representative in court	Escort	Member of the board
Immigration office chief	-	X	-	-	X
Immigration office head inspector	X	X	X	X	-
Immigration office senior inspector	X	X	X	X	-
Immigration office inspector	X	X		X	-
Immigration office head inspector	X	-	-	X	-

* the table designed by the author

Finally, a logical question may arise: who is better after all "universal soldier" or a subject matter official? There could be no short answer to it, but at the same time it is possible to determine advantages and disadvantages of their position.

Table No.5.7. **Generalist or subject matter official, advantages and disadvantages.**

	advantages	disadvantages
generalist	officials interchangeability (if necessary driver can be interpreter and vice versa)	* not deep knowledge in each position
subject matter official	deep knowledge in his position	unable to substitute colleagues in different positions

the table designed by the author

* For example, if a generalist has 8 working hours per day, then these ones may be divided : x for driving, y for interpreting, z-for bookkeeping.($x + y + z = 8$) At the same time subject matter official is responsible only for bookkeeping for entire 8 hours per day. If they have equal intensity of work and working hours then the bookkeeper should be more competent and profound in bookkeeping than the generalist and at the same time the generalist may be better than bookkeeper at driving or interpreting.

The above-mentioned hypothesis is theoretical one since there may be brilliant generalists who are as good as or even better in bookkeeping than bookkeepers, and poor bookkeepers who are worse or equal at their bookkeeping than the generalist. In order to avoid both extremities, there should be both generalists and subject matter officials at work and their proportion must be defined by a manager.

Survey No.6. **Operational interchangeability of workers**

The aim of this survey has been to find out the interchangeability of officials of one department. Interchangeability in simple words is the ability of one worker to replace the other in his job. It is hardly possible to measure the interchangeability degree of workers precisely because there are a lot of uncountable human features: character, health, mental disposition which must be considered. But then one can formulate the interchangeability degree of some elements like "fuzzy sets." (30, 23)

Table 5.8. **Interchangeability of workers in department x.**

Worker No.	Do you have driving licence?	Which is your knowledge level of foreign languages?	Do you escort detained persons?	Do you form protocols?	Book-keeping?
1	no	no	no	no	yes
2	yes	conversational	yes	no	no
3	yes	higher	yes	yes	no
4	no	no	no	yes	no
5	no	no	no	yes	no
6	yes	no	no	yes	no
7	yes	conversational	yes	yes	no
9	yes	no	yes	no	no
10	yes	no	yes	yes	no

* 10 officials has been surveyed * the table designed by the author

From this table one can see that worker No.3. is theoretically the most universal one because he is capable of completing all sorts of duties in x department, but in opposition to him there is worker No.1. who in practice is the only one responsible for a particular job at the department- drawing reports. Consequently, worker No. 1 is- the only one subject matter official and No. 3 is the generalist and the rest ones are interchangeable to a greater or lesser degree.

Survey No.7. **Sequence of actions**

The aim of this survey was to define, if possible, correct sequence of actions for an official in a situation when he has just detected a foreigner without any travel documents. Seven immigration officials have been surveyed.

Table 5.9. **Appropriate sequence of actions in the case of a foreigner without any travel documents**

Indexed actions	Officials` replies
1. to draw administrative violation protocol for staying illegally; 2. inspection report; 3. foreigner's explanation; 4. foreigner's rights and duties; 5. report to the chief; 6. ....(may be continued)	V: 3,1,2,4,5; A: 2,4,3,1,5; G: 2,3,4,1,5; P: 1,4,3,2,5; J: 4,3,1,2,5; Jr: 4,2,3,1,5, R: 4,2,3,1,5. *the average answer:* 4,2,3,1,5.

* the table designed by the author

According to the results the majority of immigration service officials in the situation of illegal immigrant would act in line with the sequence: 4, 3 or 2, 3, 1, 5. Is it correct to conclude that sequential procedures 4, 2, 3, 1, 5 may be considered as the standard and to be approved as operational instruction for immigration service officials? The answer is – accumulation of data. If a drafter of the instruction aims to compose the most appropriate instruction for official's action in a particular situation, he should survey as many officials as possible in order to take out the chain that is repeated most often.

Accumulation of data allows performing more precise analysis and draw accurate conclusions. (see the next table) But even if the best chain of action has been distinguished and inserted into a document, nevertheless, possible amendments are not excluded. One may say that it is impossible to create an ideal law or instruction, because life is more complicated than may seem and sometimes departure from the best instruction is necessary. Though, in spite of natural shortcomings of human laws, instructions, still statistical computation should be performed.

For example let us analyse two apparently similar cases: to detain Nigerian citizen x for illegal stay and to detain Nigerian citizen y for illegal stay. From the point of view of service instruction both x and y should be treated similarly as illegal immigrants from Nigeria, but in practice each case will be always unique one and consequently actions 4, 2, 3, 1, 5 are conventional ones.

In the following table one can see association between accumulation of data and their accuracy. The rule "more data- better accuracy" is in effect not only in experiments with coin, but social, legal processes as well.

Table 5.1.1. **Occurrence of "eagle" depending on flipping a coin**

coin has been flipped times	Occurrence of "eagle" times
5	0,4
50	0,47
5000	0,48
more than 5000...	0,487...

* the table designed by the author

For example if one flips a coin 5 times and eagle appears 2 times then it does not mean that eagle's probability is 40%! It was proved that both eagle and tails of the coin appear with probability up to 50% when *numerous* experiments are conducted. Considering this fact the above-mentioned chain of action 4, 2, 3, 1, 5 may not be the best one due to the insufficient number of experiments conducted by the author-only 7. And how to determine the number of conducted experiments necessary to acknowledge the fact?

The experiment No.1. Decision tree or text?

Conditions of the experiment: the border guards had been split into two groups (in threes): the first one received **adapted** text materials called ,, decision tree," but the second one- original Law.

The task for two border guard groups:

Task No.1: As fast as possible to find the appropriate paragraph of the Law defining foreigners' detention term;

Task No.2: To remember foreigner's maximum detention term;

Task No.3: To distinguish two statuses to which the maximum detention term is applied.

Table 5.1.2. **Experiment No.1. results**

Task	Average result
1.	Tie first group answered correctly in 32,3 seconds. The second one in 5,19 minutes.
2.	Tie first group: 3 borderguards-3 correct answers. The second one 3 borderguards-1 correct answer.
3.	Tie first group: 3 borderguards-3 correct answers. The second one 3 borderguards-0 correct answers.

* the table designed by the author

Table 5.1.3. **Advantages and disadvantages of decision tree**

Depending on the size and kind of the tree its advantages and disadvantages may be the following:

advantages	disadvantages
1. helps to find necessary information quickly;	1. does not encourage reading skills;
2. short, informative text is easier to memorize;	2. considerable time is necessary to make summary of laws, instructions to create decision tree.
3. summary of various laws, operating instructions;	
4. effective from pedagogical point of view- lucidity;	
5. amendable, corrigible.	

*the table designed by the author*As a result, on the one hand adapted text, which includes decision trees, is more understandable for contemporary readers, but on the other hand it has one considerable disadvantage - readers fully relying on the adapted text atrophy their reading skills gradually. Eventually they might find themselves unable to read complicated original texts, for example laws, operating instructions, rules. Inability to read is not the impotence to spell words, but inability to comprehend meaning of the text. In order to save space in the decision tree, each cell is abbreviated at most and for this reason text loses its expressiveness, becomes condensed or "dry."

Table 5.1.4. **Decision tree „possible detention terms in a case if a person without any travels documents according to Latvian laws"**

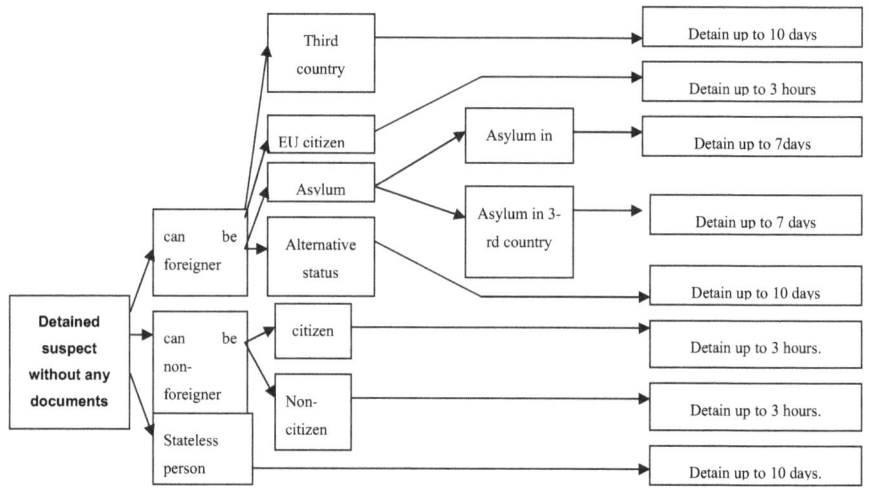

* the tree designed by the author

The experiment No.2. Correct question-half of the answer.

In this experiment participants had been separated into two groups. One group had been asked the question –*a* and the second one –*b*. B- question contains partial answer. Both groups were interviewed separately from each other in order to analyse their answers and their quality.

The situation presented to the respondents is a scenario when a detainee who is being interrogated suddenly falls on interrogator.

Question *a*	First group replies to the question a	Question *b*	Second group replies to the question b
What special means will you use in order to stop detainee assaulting you?	1. hand cuffs; 2. gas bottle; 3. physical force; 4. truncheon; 5. firearm.	What will you do to restrict detainee's hands, legs, head?	1. hand cuffs; 2. waist belt; 3. submission hold.

** the table designed by the author*Here *b* question was with the hint or partial answer already in it. *B* question reduces the number of answers but increases their quality and indeed, in order to suppress brawler's assault it is necessary to limit the parts of his body which are the fastest, most flexible and the most dangerous at that moment- his arms, legs, head. Restriction means proposed for *b* question not only suppress main threats for officials, but also reduce detainee's mortality risk during suppression procedure.

Experiment No. 3 **Morphological analysis software or experience?**

In the following experiment two contestants: morphological analysis software and the immigration service official will compete to perform the task. The task is to educe all possible deportation actions of a policeman in order to return an illegal immigrant back to Russia. (see the next table) In addition to the main task, the contestants have to allocate these actions in consecutive order.

Table 5.1.5.**Chain of actions returning an illegal immigrant.**

Symbols and their interpretations
$P(a, b, c, d,)$ – dimensions containing a,b,c,d – actions;
$P(a)$ – *desire to return* , a_1 – immigrant wants to return to his native land ,
a_2 – immigrant does not want to return to his native land;
$P(b)$ –*necessity of escort accompanying deportee* ,
b_1 – deport under escort b_2 – without escort;
$P(c)$ – *means of transport*, c_1 – by plane, c_2 – by train, c_3 – by car;
$P(d)$ – *financing return operation*, d_1 – financed by host State, d_2 – financed by EU,
d_3 – financed by the deportee;
$P(x)$ – may be continued…

* *the table designed by the author*

Table 5.1.6. **Experiment No.3 results.**

official's reply	official's response time (seconds)	morphological analysis software's replies
1. a_1,b_2,c_1,d_2. Is read as followed: if the immigrant wants to return to his native land, he flies without escort, by plane, paying for ticket himself;	40	a_1,b_2,c_1,d_1 $a_1b_2\ c_1d_2;$ $a_1\ b_1c_1d_3;$ $a_2b_2c_1d_1;$ $a_2b_1c_2d_1;$
2. $a_1b_1c_1d_1$	55	$a_2b_1c_3d_1;$
3. $a_2b_1c_2d_3$	80	....
4. $a_1b_2c_1d_1$	35	**36** variations together
5. $a_2b_1c_2d_1$. if an immigrant does not want to return to his native land, he will be deported under escort, by train, financed by State	25	

* the table designed by the author

Let us analyse the speed, quality and quantity of replies given by the software and the official. The latter produced 5 deportation scenarios for 235 seconds or 3,91 minutes ant the software, in its turn, *all* possible 36 scenarios for * 1 second! From the first glance it could seem that the software is the winner in this competition for its speed, quantity but what about the quality? The official considered only 5 ways of deporting an immigrant and due to the restricted time given for fulfilling the task, the official remembered the most frequent and acceptable scenarios from his practical experience. All official's five scenarios are more or less applicable and that can not be said about several scenarios produced by the software, for example: $a_2\ b_2\ c_2\ d_2$ which is definitely wrong reply containing contradictory actions.

Let us interpret the scenario: a_2 – immigrant refuses to return voluntarily, b_2 he will be returned without escort! c_2 – by train, d_2–financed from EU funds. The absurd variation a_2 b_2 c_2 d_2 can not be implemented because there is extra high risk that the immigrant who does not want to return to his country will escape if he is sent alone especially by train which has many stops until the border. In order to avoid the appearance of incompatible actions, software programmer must exclude simultaneous appearance of both $a_2 . b_2$. If the programmer excludes $a_2 . b_2$ chain from the software then there will be not 36, but 27 non controversial scenarios. In the above-mentioned competition the author symbolically assumed that the software calculated all possible 36 variations for 1 second but it does not matter in the least because as far back as in 1981 there were systems capable of processing information with the speed 4,7 Mgh/second, Mg- here means one million.

Human officer may effectively compete with the software in *particular* situations because he possesses intuition and human reason, features which are irreproducible ones, but when the task is too complicated containing dozens, hundred possible actions the software may be irreplaceable. Complicated task may arise when there is the necessity expelling highly dangerous criminals or terrorists. The amount of actions will increase significantly because extra tasks and precautions must be taken in consideration dealing with terrorist's deportation (see the next table). Such complicated cases are being solved as is customary: phone calls, meetings, operating instructions, debates. But the problem could have been rapidly solved applying morphological analysis software.

Table 5.1.7. **Chain of actions returning a recidivist or a terrorist.**

actions to be performed	chain of action
P (a, b, c, d,) – dimensions containing a,b,c,d...actions;	$a_1b_1c_1d_1e_1f_2g_1h_3;$
P (a) –*transportation*; a_1 – by plane a_2 – other means;	$a_1b_1c_1d_1e_2f_2g_1h_3;$
P (b) –*choosing deportation route*; b_1 – direct flight, run , b_2 –via a transit country;	$a_1b_1c_1d_1e_1f_2g_1h_2;$ Together -**374!**
P (c) –*compatibility*; c_1 – to deport separately, c_2 – together with other deportees;	
P (d) – *escort number per deportee*; d_1 – two escort members, d_2 – more than two;	
P(e) – *restriction means*; e_1 –with; e_2 – without;	
P(f) – *third persons during operation* (doctor, translator) ; f_1 – included , f_2– excluded;	
P(g) – *coordination with*; g_1 – air company, transit and destination country; g_2 –no coordination;	
P (h) – *financing return operation*, h_1 – financed by State, h_2 – financed by EU, h_3 – financed by deportee.	

* *the table designed by the author*

Survey No.8. **Reading skills among immigration service officials.**

Six immigration service officials had been given the instruction to read on how to use AFIS or automatic fingerprint identification system. After having read the instruction they were asked ten after-reading questions. (see below) The aim of the survey is to determine text comprehension level which completely depends on officials' reading skills.

1) How is AFIS abbreviation translated?

2) Whose records are inserted in AFIS?

3) Who may insert data in AFIS?

4) Which biometrical records are compared in AFIS?

5) With which information system does AFIS perform data exchange?

6) Who supervises AFIS?

7) Which records are inserted in AFIS?

8) Who may receive AFIS records?

9) After how many years the inserted records may be put into archive software?

10) How long AFIS records are stored in the system?

Table 5.1.8. **Officials' replies**

question No.	Mr. R	Mr. J	Mrs. J.	Mr. M.	Mr. S	Mr. V
1	-	-	-	-	-	-
2	-	+	-	+	+	+
3	-	+	+	+	+	-
4	+	+	+	+	+	+
5	+	+	-	+	+	+
6	-	+	-	+	+	+
7	+-	+	-	+	-	-
8	-	+	+	+	+-	-
9	+	+	+	+	+	+
10	-	+	-	+	+	+
wrong answers	6	1	6	1	2	4

* the table designed by the author

Keys: + means correct answer, - wrong answer, + - partly correct answer. As a result only three officials were able to read and comprehend the instruction: J, M, S.

Experiment No. 4. **The ability to find necessary instruction.**

The *aim* of this experiment is to observe officials' actions in real work situations. Due to the huge torrent of information and its inappropriate storage and upgrade in immigration service the author perceived natural embarrassment and confusion in abnormal situations when officials must take quick and responsible decisions. Necessary operating instructions, rules, laws are usually kept in paper folders or maps. An official, of course, can not remember all relevant instruction and maps serve here as reference, storage of information. It can happen that a probative commission may arrive unexpectedly to the office and checks an official on duty his actions in response to different situations (fire alarm, asylum seeker afflux, blast and so on) There are a lot of different situations and an official has to respond adequately and rapidly according to the operating instructions. An official can be working efficiently in ordinary and predictable situations and may be confused in unexpected and unpredictable ones. Due to the constant amendments of operating instructions, laws, even customary actions may become challenging for officials.

In this experiment the author played the role of a controller and an official - the examinee. The following question concerning asylum seeker's procedure had been asked: "on which basis officials are allowed to record interview with asylum seeker"? The author notices that the official starts to think, but then turns to the maps and finds asylum seekers law where he skims it for key words. After some minutes, he pronounces the correct article of asylum law. And that was training alert. But what would happen if it had not been a training alert? While searching for reply there could appear official's nervousness, fuss and vanity if it had been in reality. Such unnecessary fuss could have been excluded if an official managed software program with *actual, accessible* laws, instructions with the function of search engine.

CHAPTER 6

The *aim* of the paper was to distinguish the factors decreasing the risks while taking decision in immigration service of the State border guard. The decision is taken by a border guard who at the same time is the official. In the overwhelming majority of the cases border guards' decision will depend on what is written in laws, rules and operating instructions in other words they determine his legal, procedural actions. As all legislation is presented in the written text, it should be read and understood subsequently. Comprehension of the text will determine subsequent decisions - correct or the wrong one. Reading is not simply spelling the words, but uppermost it is: memorizing, comparing, drawing conclusions. Since not all officials are able to read, there may be designed adaptive, supplementary summaries such as decision trees, morphological tables which may substitute original text. Supplementary materials are distinctive in their thoroughness, for example, on the average decision tree's one A4 page may contain summary of vital information that is extracted from the original text with volume on some pages.

Another effective the way of summarization is morphological analysis which reveals *all* possible combinations from the data given. It is especially usable in the cases when there is too much information being processed. Both decision tree and morphological analysis may be created manually on paper, on chalkboard or developed in software application.

The *tasks* of this work are to define risk factors, to analyse how risk influences decision taking, to find out risk decreasing factors, to apply to risk decreasing factors in practice. Risk factors which induce wrong decision-making are the following: poor reading skills (survey No.8), great quantity of information and its poor arrangement (experiment No.4). Survey No. 2 indicates that each borderguard reads averagely 3,85 hours per week, watches TV 1,68 hours per week and only 3 of 8 officials write letters by hand. As the result legal text is almost incomprehensible for majority of contemporary readers.

The following words and their antonyms like for example: similar-dissimilar, risky-safe, much-little, sufficient-insufficient which are frequent parts of sentences and normally used in general sense, rhetorically in official letters, reports, nevertheless may possess decisive value in mathematics, statistics because threshold degree inserted into the comparison algorithm of recognition software strictly discerns who is similar or dissimilar, risky or safe. A person being recognized as similar to the wanted one requires adequate treatment from the law enforcement authorities; therefore there is necessity to define threshold degree accurately in order to minimize possible risks.

Chapter 3 of the paper reveals adequate solutions to the parameterization of the decisive algorithm - $r*$. If speaking about the factors which decrease possibility of errors committed by an official, they are opposite to those of the increasing ones: good reading skills, adequate arrangement of information (decision trees, summaries of operating instructions, laws, tables, adaptive text, morphological analysis and so on). Successful implementation of risk decreasing factors in practice occurred in the experiments No.1 (decision tree) and No.3 (morphological analysis).

Hypothesis

Author's adduced argument that systematization of actions decreases the probability to take incorrect decision in immigration service work proved to be genuine. Definition of the term -system, according to the dictionary is parts "located in interrelation" regularly. (38) Immigration service official's actions are subjected to the relevant laws and operating instructions, the latter ones after having been systematized, summarized and adapted proved to be more comprehensible for their users. Moreover, the systematization decreases decision taking time and improves decision's quality. The author of the paper tried to systemize and summarize some of the actual laws and operating instructions according to logic, probability, risk and decision taking theories. As a result, the author designed morphological tables, decision trees. For example, in order to design the decision tree - "to detain a foreigner" complying with the statutory requirements, it is necessary to read, aggregate and summarize the following laws: Immigration law, Code of Administrative procedure and Alien's law. The final product of this aggregation - the decision tree proved to be efficient (experiment No.1.) As a result, users could both find particular information faster and remembered the content better. Optimistic results of the experiment No.1. did not enchant the author because users of adaptive materials should contend with the fact that there will always be consequent "pitfall" - degeneration of reading skills.

At the same time the decision tree designed for usage is handy and expedient means providing its user with the summary of vital parts of law, instruction and often it is not extensive in order to be observable and readable. If there is necessary to distinguish all combinations possible there is necessary to apply morphological analysis method. Usually it is extensive and should be processed in the software. As for immigration service work, morphological analysis is applicable to discern all possible officials' actions in appropriate, logical succession. For example, in experiment No.3 there were represented all possible actions necessary to deport a foreigner out of the country. Another   kind   of systematization or better to say the systematization of one's mind is the method of putting correct question. To put correct question means to ask the one which already contains half answer inside. (experiment No.2.)

While completing the present paper the author faced the following difficulties: the references on the subject of risk assessment, decision, probability theory, morphological analysis were mostly not related to jurisdiction but to economy, science.

In our "button" century that is characterized with misbalance between increasing torrent of information and decreasing time to process it. As a result there is a huge demand for adaptation of the torrent to the needs of their users. (experiment No. 4) The author intentionally applied the verb *users* not readers because contemporary man reads less and less, but watches more and more and such tendency leads to degeneration of reading skills. (survey No.3). As all laws and operating instructions are written, they must be read and understood properly, otherwise misunderstanding may cause severe consequences. As the possible solution could be the decision making software which provides its users with updated, accessible information for a particular situation. And according to survey No. 2 all quizzed immigration service officials expressed the desire to implement adapted interpretations of law and operating instructions which in its turn is quite clear indication of the current problem: general inability to read original text from one hand and unsatisfied demand for adaptive systems.

Another topic touched in the paper is person identification. Most of the developed countries for the purpose of person identification implement computer software comparing person's biometrical data. But biometrical database works according to algorithms inserted into the system by its designers, and therefore here arises eternal question: "where is the border between hits: recognized-unrecognized, wanted-not wanted, guilty-innocent? How to measure it? According to the survey led by the author, the officials think that this border starts from 78 %, in other words, there must be similarity, correlation degree not less than 78% between two samples to consider them identical (survey No.4).

In the present paper the author has also investigated the side effects of implementation of adapted materials, decision software that is expressed in degeneration of reading, logical skills. As the possible solution to this problem there could be regular tasks and assignments on decision making with exclusion of all adapted materials and backup software.

SUGGESTIONS

1. To create the *service* whose officials would be fully occupied in adapting, summarizing laws, operating instructions and sustaining decision making data base.

2. To conduct regular tasks and assignments on decision making.

3. To consider the possibility to use $r*$ algorithm in the software.

4. To implement person recognition software respecting human rights for freedom and avoiding excessive checks.

REFERENCES

1) Aladdin M. Yaqub. An Introduction to Logical Theory. Broadview Press, 2013.
2) Alan Axelrod. The Real History of World War II: A New Look at the Past. Sterling Publishing Co, 2008.
3) Alan L. Porter, Scott W. Cunningham, Jerry Banks, A. Thomas Roper, Thomas W. Mason, Frederick A. Rossini. Forecasting and Management of Technology. John Wiley & Sons, 2011.
4) Alberto Brugnoli. Dangerous Materials: Control, Risk Prevention and Crisis Management.Springer, 2010.
5) Andre Ponce de Leon F. de Carvalho, Sara Rodríguez-González. Distributed Computing and Artificial Intelligence: 7th International Symposium. Springer, 2010.
6) Anil K. Jain, Arun Abraham Ross, Karthik Nandakumar. Introduction to Biometrics. Springer, 2011.
7) Barbara Kroll. Second Language Writing: Research Insights for the Classroom. Cambridge University Press, 1990.
8) Berger Vance. The Probability Problem Solver: A Complete Solution Guide to Any Textbook. Research & Education Association, 2001.
9) Bigün Josef, Gustavsson Tomas. Image analysis: 13th Scandinavian conference. Halmstad, Sweden: SCIA,2003.
10) Bok Derek. Our Underachieving Colleges: A Candid Look at How Much Students Learn and Why They Should Be Learning More. Princeton University Press,1997.
11) Brendan Kelly. Statistics with the TI-83 Plus & TI-83 Plus SE. Brendan Kelly Publishing Inc.2002.
12) Bruce F. Baird. Managerial Decisions under Uncertainty: An Introduction to the Analysis of Decision Making. Wiley-Interscience, 1989.
13) Brunsson Nils. The consequences of decision making. Oxford University Press Inc., New York, 2007.
14) Cerrito Patricia B. Introduction of data mining using SAS Interprise Miner. SAS publishing, 2007.
15) Charles E. Baukal Jr. Oxygen-Enhanced Combustion, Second Edition. CRC Press, 2013.
16) Christoph Schiller. Motion Mountain - vol. 6 - The Strand Model - A Speculation on Unification. Christoph Schiller, 2012.
17) Connie Juel. Learning to Read and Write in One Elementary School.Springer-Verlag New Yourk Inc, 1994.
18) Daft Richard L. Organization Theory and Design. South-Western, 2006.
19) David Ruelle. Chance and Chaos. Princenton University Press, 1991.
20) De Ville Barry. Decision trees for business intelligence and data mining: using SAS Enterprise Miner. SAS Press Series, 2006.
21) Dewitt B. Lucas. Handwriting & Character Analysis. Health research, 1996.
22) Dhiren R. Patel. Information Security: Theory and Practice. Prentice-Hall, 2008.
23) Dominic Palmer-Brown. Engineering Applications of Neural Networks, Dominic Palmer-Brown – 2009.
24) Dorn James A. The future of money in the infrmation age. Cato Institute, 1997.
25) Edward E. Hueske. Firearms and Fingerprints.Facts on File Inc., 2009.

26) Emblemsvagn Jan. Life-Cycle costing. John Wiley & Sons, 2003.
27) Françoise Bouchet-Saulnie. The Practical Guide to Humanitarian Law. Rowman & Littlefield Pub.Inc. 2007.
28) Genrich Altshuller. The Innovation Algorithm: TRIZ, Systematic Innovation and Technical Creativity. Technical Innovation Center, Inc, 1999.
29) Gerhard Müller, Michael Möser. Handbook of Engineering Acoustics. Springer, 2012.
30) Gloria Bordogna, Gabriella Pas. Recent Issues on Fuzzy Databases. Springer, 2000.
31) Goodwyn Andrew. English in the digital age: information and communications technology. London: Cassell, 1999.
32) Gregory H. Duckert. Practical Enterprise Risk Management: A Business Process Approach. John Wiley & Sons, 2011.
33) Hanssonn. S.V. Decision theory.A brief introduction. Minor revisions. Stockholm, 2005.
34) Harry Wechsler. Reliable Face Recognition Methods: System Design, Implementation and Evaluation. Springer, 2009.
35) Horowitz. Ira. Organization and decision theory. Kluwer Academic Publishers, Boston : 1990.
36) Hossein Bidgoli. Handbook of Information Security, Threats, Vulnerabilities, Prevention, Detection and Management. John Wiley & Sons, 2009.
37) http://en.wikipedia.org/wiki/SAS_(software). Software.
38) http://tsisa.ru/history. Morfoloģiska analīze.
39) http://www.vvc.gov.lv/export/sites/default/docs/LRTA/Likumi/Immigration_Law.doc.Latvian immigration Law.
40) Jean M. Twenge. eneration Me: Why Today's Young Americans Are More Confident, Assertive Entitled and More Miserable Than Ever Before. Simon and Schuster, 2006.
41) John R. Vacca. Biometric Technologies and Verification Systems,
42) John Riordan. Introduction to Combinatorial Analysis.Unabridged Dover, 2002.
43) Jon M. Shane. What Every Chief Executive Should Know: Using Data to Measure Police Performance. Jon M. Shane, 2007.
44) Joseph J. Feher. Quantitative Human Physiology: An Introduction. Elsevier Enc.2012.
45) Leslie Edwards. Practical Risk Management in the Construction Industry. Thomas Telfold, 1995.
46) Marcus Galdia. Legal Linguistics. Peter Lang GmbH, 2009.
47) Mark Stamp. Handbook of Information and Communication Security. Springer, 2010.
48) Massimo Tistarelli, S. Z. Li, Rama Chellappa. Handbook of Remote Biometrics: for Surveillance and Security. Springer 2009.
49) Mathematics Accomplished: The Year 6 Booster. BEAM Eduacation 2001.
50) Michael L. Radelet. In Spite of Innocence: Erroneous Convictions in Capital Cases. UPNE, 1994.
51) Michelle J. Kelley, Nicki Clausen-Grace. Comprehension Shouldn't Be Silent: From Strategy Instruction to Student. International Reading Assoc, 2013.
52) Mundsack Allan, Deese James, Deese Ellin . How to Study 5/e. James Deese, 2002.
53) Nadler Gerald, William J. Chandon. Smart questions: learn to ask the right questions for powerful results. Jossey-Bass,2004

54) Ohsuga Setsuo. Information modelling and knowledge bases. Eds. IOS Press, 1992.
55) Orasanu Judith. Reading Comprehension: From Research to Practice. USA Hillsdale: Lawrence Erlbaum Associates, 1986.
56) Paul Moliken. Growing Your Vocabulary: Learning from Latin and Greek Roots - Book B.Prestwick House Inc.,2008.
57) Paula McCoy Pinderhughes. How to be an Entrepreneur and Keep Your Sanity. Paula McCoy Pinderhughes, 2004.
58) Rayner Keith, Pollatsek Alexander. The Psychology of Reading. USA Prentice-Hall: Lawrence Erlbaum, 1994.
59) Ritchey, T. General Morphological Analysis: A General Method for Non-Quantified Modelling, 2002.
60) Sousa David. How the Brain Learns to Read. USA Thousand Oaks: Corwin Press, 2004.
61) Stephen Doyle. Understanding Information Technology. Nelson Thornes, 2000.
62) Steve Davis. Cengage Advantage Books: Think Like an Editor, 2nd ed. Cengage Learning, 2012.
63) Tom Ritchey. Wicked Problems-Social Messes: Decision Support Modelling with Morphological analysis. Springer 2011.
64) Verhoeven Ludo, Elbro Carsten, Reitsma Pieter.Precursors of functional literacy, 2002.
65) Watts Taffe Susan, Carolyn B Gwin. Integrating Literacy and Technology: Effective Practice for Grades K-6.The Guilford Press,1997.
66) Wayne Michael Hall, Gary Citrenbaum. Intelligence Analysis: How to Think in Complex Environments. ABC-CLIO, 2009.
67) William J. Stewart. Probability, Markov Chains, Queues, and Simulation: The Mathematical Basis. Princenton University Press, 2009.
68) Wise Jessie, Buffington Sara. The Ordinary Parent's Guide to Teaching Reading. USA Charles City: Peace Hill Press, 2004.
69) Woods Charles Arthur, Sergile Florence E. Biogeography of the West Indies: patterns and perspectives. Crc Press, 2001.
70) Колмогоров А.Н., Журбенко И.Г.,.Прохоров А.В. Введение в теорию вероятностей. Москва:Наука,1988. 28 стр.
71) Кушнерук С.П.. Документальная лингвистика.Волгоград:Волгоградский Государственный Университет,1998.
72) Растригин.Л. Этот случайный,случайный,случайный мир.Молодая Гвардия, 1974.
73) http://en.wikipedia.org/wiki/Biometrics. False acceptance in biometry.